Poland

Postcommunist States and Nations

Books in the series

Belarus: a denationalized nation
David R. Marples

Armenia: at the crossroads
Joseph R. Masih and Robert O. Krikorian

Poland: the conquest of history
George Sanford

Kyrgyzstan: central asia's island of democracy?
John Anderson

This book is part of a series. The publisher will accept continuation orders which may be cancelled at any time and which provide for automatic billing and shipping of each title in the series upon publication. Please write for details.

Poland

THE CONQUEST OF HISTORY

George Sanford

harwood academic publishers
Australia • Canada • China • France
Germany • India • Japan • Luxembourg • Malaysia
The Netherlands • Russia • Singapore • Switzerland

Amsteldijk 166
1st Floor
1079 LH Amsterdam
The Netherlands

British Library Cataloguing in Publication Data

Sanford, George
  Poland: the conquest of history – (Postcommunist states & nations v. 3)
  1. Poland – History 2. Poland – Economic conditions
  3. Poland – Economic policy 4. Poland – Foreign relations
  I. Title
  947.8'086

  ISBN 90-5702-346-6 (hardcover)
  ISSN 1028-043X

TABLE OF CONTENTS

CHRONOLOGY

Pre-1989

966	Mieszko I of the Piast dynasty adopts Christianity
1386	Jagiello's marriage to Jadwiga inaugurates the Jagiellonian dynasty which rules until 1572
1410	The Polish-Lithuanian alliance smashes the Teutonic Knights at the battle of Grunwald
1505	*Nihil Novi* statute establishes parliamentary (Sejm) limits on royal power
1569	Union of Lublin formalises the Polish-Lithuanian Commonwealth
1572–1764	The nobility and gentry (*Szlachta*) elect monarchs mainly from the Vaza and Saxon dynasties
1683	Jan Sobieski defeats the Turks at Vienna
1772	First Partition of Poland
1791	Constitution of Third of May
1793	Second Partition
1794	Kościuszko's Uprising
1795	Poland expunged from map of Europe by Third Partition
1807–13	Grand Duchy of Warsaw
1815–30	The Congress Kingdom
1830–31	November Uprising is suppressed after war with Russia
1863–64	Russia puts down the January Uprising
1918	Poland regains independence on 11 November
1920	Piłsudski defeats Bolsheviks in front of Warsaw in August
1921	Promulgation of democratic constitution of 17 March
1926	May *coup* by Piłsudski inaugurates growing authoritarian rule
1935	An authoritarian constitution is passed in April; Piłsudski dies in May
1939	Poland is invaded by Nazi Germany on 1 September and the USSR on 17 September; she is divided up on the basis of the Ribbentrop-Molotov Pact
1940	Soviet massacre of interned Polish army officers at 'Katyń'
1944	Anders corps fights for Monte Cassino in Spring; Warsaw Uprising of August–September; Polish Committee of National Liberation becomes the Provisional Government in late December
1945	Red Army occupation and establishment of communist rule within new frontiers on the Oder-Neisse in the west and the Curzon Line in the east
1947	Rigged elections and elimination of remaining opposition
1948	Gomułka's downfall; Stalinist domination under Bierut and Rokossowski
1956	Poznań Uprising in June and popular unrest brings Gomułka back to power in October
1968	Student and reform opposition is crushed by the Anti-Zionist purge and the March Events
1970	West German recognition of the Oder-Neisse line; demonstrations on the Baltic seacoast are suppressed; Gierek replaces Gomułka

1976	Period of growing prosperity and *detente* ends: food price-increase is abandoned after Radom and Ursus riots. Their suppression leads to dissidence and the Workers' Defense Committee
1979	First visit to Poland by Pope John Paul II
1980	Growing protests during the summer against the food price-rise culminate in August sit-in strikes in the Baltic dockyards: Gdańsk, Szczecin and Jastrzębie Agreements concede rights to strike and to organise free trades unions; emergence of Solidarity led by Wałęsa
1981	Consumer collapse and socio-economic discontent: the PZPR and Solidarity hold their congresses; Jaruzelski assumes party as well as state power; the Military Council of National Salvation declares the State of War and suppresses opposition in December
1982	Organisation of underground counter-society
1983	State of War ends: Pope John Paul II visits Poland for a second time
1986	General amnesty: Jaruzelski establishes Consultative Council and Wałęsa the Solidarity Provisional Council
1987	Close failure of referendum
1988	Spring and summer strikes encourage PZPR August plenum to initiate reform course; Wałęsa sets up Civic Committee in December

Post-1989

1989

January	PZPR plenum confirms reform leadership and decision to negotiate with the opposition
6 Feb–5 April	Round Table negotiations
April	Re-legalisation of Solidarity
June	PZPR is defeated in the Sejm and Senate elections within the confines of the Round Table contract
July	Jaruzelski is barely elected as president
August	Mazowiecki is nominated as prime minister
September	Sejm confirms the Solidarity-led coalition government with communist participation; signing of EEC trade and economic agreement
December	Revision of constitution to exclude PZPR's leading-role

1990

January	Dissolution of PZPR and formation of SdRP and PUS; initiation of Balcerowicz' economic shock therapy
Summer	Resignation of communist ministers: 'war at the top' splits Solidarity
November	Polish-German Treaty confirms inviolability of their frontier: Tymiński eliminates Mazowiecki in first ballot of presidential election
December	Wałęsa elected as president

1991

January	Bielecki replaces Mazowiecki as prime minister
February	Signing of Višegrad Agreement; Solidarity Congress elects Krzaklewski as national chairman
October	First fully free election produces a fragmented Sejm

December	Olszewski appointed prime minister of a centre-right government; signing of EEC agreement on associate membership

1992

May	Timetable for withdrawal of Soviet troops in Poland agreed
June	Interior minister Macierewicz' attempts to release secret files leads to Olszewski's fall. Pawlak is nominated, but not confirmed, as prime minister
July	Suchocka forms a Solidarity orientated coalition
November	Promulgation of Little Constitution

1993

May	Wałęsa dissolves Sejm after Suchocka loses vote of confidence
September	Last operational Soviet troops leave Poland
October	SLD and PSL win a large majority of seats in Sejm election while Solidarity, KL-D, PC and the national-Catholics are excluded
November	Pawlak leads an SdRP-PSL coalition government

1994

February	Poland joins Partnership for Peace
April	Formal amalgamation of UD with KL-D to form Freedom Union (UW)
May	Borowski is replaced by Kołodko as minister of finance
June	Local Government elections
July	Wałęsa signs Treaty with Lithuania in Vilnius

1995

March	Oleksy replaces Pawlak as prime minister: Zych becomes Sejm-Marshal
April	UW Congress elects Balcerowicz as leader in place of Mazowiecki
November	In the presidential election Wałęsa heads off challenges by Kuroń, Gronkiewicz-Waltz and Olszewski but is just defeated by Kwaśniewski on the second ballot
December	Interior minister Milczanowski accuses Oleksy of betraying state secrets

1996

March	Cimoszewicz takes over as prime minister on Oleksy's resignation
April	Suspension of investigation against Oleksy
May	Attempted closure of Gdańsk shipyard
July	Sejm postpones ratification of Concordat
October	Publication of White Book on Oleksy affair
November	Bugaj's Sejm Commission report closes Oleksy affair
Winter	Reform of central ministries continues

1997

February	Belka takes over from Kołodko as minister of finance; PSL congress forces Jagieliński to resign as minister of agriculture
March	Wilecki is dismissed as Chief of Staff; Gdańsk shipyard reprieved after violent demonstration in Warsaw

April	Sejm passes constitution despite rightist and clerical opposition: AWS elects its co-ordinating committee
May	Referendum barely approves constitution on low turnout
June	Pope John Paul II makes his fifth papal visit to Poland; EU Amsterdam summit decides to begin negotiations for full membership entry with Poland
July	Serious flooding causes loss of life and vast damage in southern and western Poland; EU Commission report endorses Poland as a potential full member: Madrid summit agrees that negotiations for Poland's membership of NATO should start in 1998
September	AWS gains 202 seats on 33.8% of the vote to the SLD's 164 seats (27.1%) and the UW's 60 seats (13.4%). The PSL collapses (27 seats, 7.3%), the UP does not qualify while ROP barely does so
October	Professor Jerzy Buzek forms an AWS-UW coalition government but Krzaklewski remains a powerful force outside it
December	The influential minister of finance, Balcerowicz launches an economic austerity programme to cut the export deficit and restore financial balance

GLOSSARY OF ABBREVIATIONS

AK	Armia Krajowa: Home Army
AWS	Akcja Wyborcza 'Solidarność': Solidarity Electoral Action
BBWR	Bezpartyjny Blok Wspierania Reform: Non-Party Bloc for Supporting the Reforms
GUS	Główny Urząd Statystyczny: Main Statistical Office
KL-D	Kongres Liberalno-Demokratyczny: Liberal-Democratic Congress
KOR	Komitet Obrony Robotników: Workers' Defense Committee
KPN	Konfederacja Polski Niepodległej: Confederation for an Independent Poland
MON	Ministerstwo Obrony Narodowej: Ministry of National Defense
MSW	Ministerstwo Spraw Wewnętrznych: Ministry of Internal Affairs
MSZ	Ministerstwo Spraw Zagranicznych: Ministry of Foreign Affairs
OKP	Obywatelski Klub Parlamentarny: Civic Parliamentary Club
OPZZ	Ogólnopolskie Porozumienie Związków Zawodowych: All-Poland Alliance of Trade Unions
PAN	Polska Akademia Nauk: Polish Academy of Sciences
PC	Partia (Porozumienie) Centrum: Centre Party (Agreement)
PKWN	Polski Komitet Wyzwolenia Narodowego: Polish Committee of National Liberation
PPS	Polska Partia Socjalistyczna: Polish Socialist Party
PR	Polska Rzeczpospolita: Polish Republic
PRL	Polska Rzeczpospolita Ludowa: Polish People's Republic
PRiTV	Polska Radio i Telewizja: Polish Radio and Television
PSL	Polskie Stronnictwo Ludowe: Polish Peasant Party
PUS	Polska Unia Socjaldemokratyczna: Polish Social Democratic Union
PZPR	Polska Zjednoczona Partia Robotnicza: Polish United Workers Party
ROAD	Ruch Obywatelski 'Akcja Demokratyczna': Civic Movement 'Democratic Action'
ROP	Ruch Odbudowy Polski: Movement for Rebuilding Poland
SD	Stronnictwo Demokratyczne: Democratic Movement
SdRP	Socjaldemokracja Rzeczpospolitej Polskiej: Social Democracy of the Polish Republic
SLD	Sojusz Lewicy Demokratycznej: Alliance of the Democratic Left
SN	Stronnictwo Narodowe: National Party
UD	Unia Demokratyczna: Democratic Union
UW	Unia Wolności: Freedom Union
UOP	Urząd Ochrony Państwa: Office of State-Protection
UP	Unia Pracy: Labour Union
UPR	Unia Polityki Realnej: Union of Real Politics
URM	Urząd Rady Ministrów: Office of the Council of Ministers
WAK	Wyborcza Akcja Katolicka: Catholic Electoral Action
WRON	Wojskowa Rada Ocalenia Narodowego: Military Council of National Salvation
ZCh-N	Zjednoczenie Chrześcijańsko-Narodowe: Christian National Union
ZSL	Zjednoczone Stronnictwo Ludowe: United Peasant Party

Map of Poland

Chapter 1

FROM 'GOD'S PLAYGROUND' TO NORMALITY

Situated in the centre of Europe between Germany and Russia, Poland's geographical position has contributed to an especially turbulent history in modern times. The loss of national independence and partition by three powerful neighbours from 1795–1918, partial modernisation during the interwar period and Nazi occupation and genocide during the Second World War culminated in massive population transfers and boundary changes at its end. Postwar Poland, now ethnically homogeneous and overwhelmingly Roman Catholic, then underwent the Soviet form of socio-economic trans-formation under conditions of limited sovereignty. Communist rule was, however, profoundly affected by repeated social and political challenges; these were both evolutionary and open, as in the crises of 1956, 1968, 1970 and 1976, with the emergence of Solidarity in 1980–81. Since 1989 Poland has been building a new democratic system and has rejoined the world cap-italist economy and the European framework of integration and mutual security concerns. Poland contributed enormously to the downfall of com-munism. Its experience produced a wide-ranging political and academic lit-erature on communist reform, collapse and successor development. The chances for the continued survival of the country's special cultural and national features in an age of triumphant democratic capitalism, European-ism and globalisation will be examined in this volume.

One cannot hope to summarise over a thousand years in a great nation's history in detail in a short chapter.[1] But one can identify some of the main events, as well as the themes which are perceived by Poles today as instruct-ive and meaningful to their current situation. In that sense, Poland's history still has consequences for its post-communist politics, society and general intel-lectual and political consciousness. It is a long established tradition that Poles debate and assess contemporary problems through the prism of their recurrent historical and geostrategic dilemmas. One can identify such issues as whether national priority should be given to a Western or Eastern orientation and whether active responses should be preferred to passivity; there has been a heart-searching national debate from the eighteenth century onwards about the relationship between domestic and external politics and the former's respons-ibility for Poland's decline, partition and loss of independence. The sense of drama and tragedy in Poland's history and politics is undoubtedly great, but it is by no means unique in the East European experience. It has, however, been propagated by authors whose titles such as *The Polish Volcano* (Flora Lewis), *God's Playground* (Norman Davies) and *Bridge for the Abyss* (Richard Hiscocks) scream this theme at the reader.

The great Polish historian Oskar Halecki made the following, still pertinent, observations in his classic history written during the Second World War. Although the particulars of Poland's turbulent thousand year history are imbedded as vital elements in the national psyche, many key features are still largely unknown abroad opening the way for unsubstantiated, and often unjust, judgements. Can an outsider hope to understand Poland's great power mentality without knowing anything of the Polish–Lithuanian Commonwealth? Lumping the *historic* nation of Poland, comparable to Spain, together with smaller and newer states because of partial glimpses of the unhappy periods in her past such as that of the partitions distorts understanding even more than outright ignorance [Introduction to Halecki 1978]. It is as misleading to assess Poland's current regional policy in Eastern Europe without taking these factors on board as it would be to neglect Britain's imperial and pro-American past in explaining her erratic relationship with the European Union (EU). One should also beware of the cumulative effect of the historical propaganda of Poland's enemies depicting the Poles as troublesome national and social revolutionaries during the partition period and unbalanced megalomaniacs subsequently. Even self-interested critiques may contain a measure of truth, but the prime need is for an understanding of the varied idealist and realist responses during the last two centuries to Poland's geopolitical dilemma of regaining independence and then ensuring survival between normally hostile and much stronger Russian and German powers. Judgements on the democratic and modernisation potential of interwar Poland and the lessons assimilated by modern Poles from that experience need to be contrasted with the survival dilemma and the long-lasting effects of brutal Nazi occupation during the Second World War. A major account of the Warsaw Uprising in the Summer of 1944 concludes that its main long-term consequence was the predominance of cautious and realist attitudes in communist Poland towards uprisings and loss of life until a new generation set a very different tone after 1980.[2] The prospects for the successful entrenchment of democratic capitalism and full integration in Europe have also largely been discussed in the form of a lively, and continuing, debate on the communist experience and its consequences. These points have been re-iterated by Norman Davies who deserves much credit for re-integrating neglected aspects of the Polish and East European experience into the wider West European and Atlanticist consciousness.[3] Due weight will, however, also be given to the modernisation argument in this study as a set-off to the historical and geo-strategic themes; the collapse of Soviet hegemony and communist rule in Eastern Europe means that Poland's national history can now be viewed as 'an integral part of European history' in the balanced sense which Halecki originally intended [Halecki 1978, p. ix].

FOUNDATION MYTHS: PIAST POLAND

The origins of the Poles are still the subject of considerable historical debate. What is clear is that the Poles developed out of the western linguistic branch (along with the Czechs and Slovaks) of the larger three branched, southern and eastern, Slav family by about the ninth century AD. The *Polanie* (dwellers of the field or plain) together with closely similar Mazovian, Pomeranian and Silesian groups settled in what became the core of the Polish heartland bounded by the river Oder (Odra) and stretching over the basin of the river Vistula (Wisła) to the east and as far as the Carpathian mountains to the south. The successful ruling dynasty was established by the eponymious, if somewhat mythical, Piast some generations before the emergence of Poland onto the European stage; in 966 a successor, Mieszko I, accepted Christianity on marrying a Bohemian princess in order to gain support against the Germans.[4] Polish state sovereignty was thus from the outset linked firmly to Roman Catholicism.

Poland was christianised quickly by Mieszko, who sought Papal support against both German and Russian incursions. His successor Bolesław I *Chrobry* (the Brave) established an independent Polish church linked to Rome with its own archbishop at Gniezno in 1000. He repelled the Germans, rounded off the Polish state by conquering territory as far as Kiev and achieved full state sovereignty by being crowned king just before his death in 1025. His successors were unable to prevent the feudal disintegration of the kingdom but the Polish heartland of Greater Poland (Wielkopolska) was largely maintained despite continual incursions by Mongol hordes, notably in the great invasion of 1241, and by the Teutonic Knights after 1226. The latter led to the loss of the northern Baltic seacoast and Pomerania. These factors contributed to the emergence of Kraków as the national capital by around 1300. The last Piast king, Kazimierz III the Great (1330–1370), as well as reconsolidating the state, fostered economic and cultural life, established East-Central Europe's second oldest university in Kraków in 1364 and sought compensation in alliance with Bohemia and Hungary for losses to the Germans in eastward expansion as far as Lwów.[5] Subsequent perceptions of Piast Poland were to crystallise around the concept of an ethnically compact heartland on the Vistula and Warta rivers with the primary Germanic enemy threatening the Oder frontier and the Baltic seacoast while southern alliances ensured security and moderate expansion to the east.[6]

JAGIELLONIAN POLAND AND THE POLISH–LITHUANIAN COMMONWEALTH

Poles consider the fifteenth and sixteenth centuries to have been a Golden Age in their history—a time which saw much 'greatness and glory'.[7] Poland achieved its maximum international greatness while domestically a stable political system allowed cultural, social and economic life to flourish. The replacement of the southern option by an eastern one, after the extinction of the Piast dynasty in 1370, had enormous consequences for both the country's international standing as well as its domestic composition. The marriage of Jadwiga (reigned 1383–99) to the Lithuanian Grand Duke who converted to Catholicism and ruled as King Władysław II Jagiełło (1386–1434) had dramatic consequences for Poland. The combined Polish–Lithuanian forces smashed the Teutonic Order in 1410, in what the Poles consider to be their most celebrated victory, at Grunwald (Tannenberg in German); but sloppy diplomacy delayed the final regaining of Pomerania and the Baltic seacoast until the Treaty of Toruń of 1466. It was only in 1525 that the Order finally transformed itself into the secular Duchy of Prussia under Hohenzollern rule paying homage to the Polish Crown.

The Jagiellonian dynasty expanded eastwards most notably under Kazimierz IV (1444–92) and his successors. At its peak the joint Polish–Lithuanian state controlled the bulk of what are now the Baltic States, Belarus and the Ukraine stretching as far as Smolensk and occupying the *międzymorze* between the Baltic and Black Seas, a regional concept that long remained powerfully imprinted in the Polish historical consciousness. But it never succeeded in regaining Silesia and West Pomerania while its incursions into Transylvania and Moldavia were short-lived. The massive and territorially far-flung Jagiellonian state was not only much less compact than its Piast predecessor but also far more ethnically and religiously diverse. The personal dynastic union suffered from much friction between the Polish and Lithuanian components. But it also produced a fine tradition of religious tolerance and political compromise. A magnificent Renaissance flowering of the arts and culture occurred (symbolised by the astronomer Nicholas Copernicus, the historian Jan Długosz and the humanist writers Jan Kochanowski and Mikołaj Rej) combined with great commercial expansion and economic prosperity under kings Zygmunt I the Old (1506–48) and Zygmunt II

Augustus (1548–72). The Jagiellonian dynasty died out with the latter. This was preceded by the Union of Lublin of 1569 which amalgamated Poland and Lithuania into the Commonwealth of Both Nations known as the *Rzeczpospolita* (Republic). The nobility and its large supporting gentry group (*szlachta*) came to dominate the state by electing the monarch from 1572 onwards and by controlling parliament, the Senate and the Sejm (lower house), as well as the local parliaments (*Sejmiki*).[8]

The institution of elective monarchy, despite the successful, but regrettably short, reign of Stefan I Batory of Transylvania (1575–86), proved disastrous for Poland. Successful candidates bargained for support by promising privileges to the nobility in the form of a *Pacta Conventa*. This weakened the central executive power irreversibly producing a decentralised form of estates-democracy. After 1587 Poland also fell into the hands of three successive Vaza kings who involved her in unnecessary and damaging dynastic and religious wars with Sweden. They moved the capital to Warsaw by 1611 but overstretched the Commonwealth's resources in an attempt to gain dynastic control of Muscovy in 1607–13. The compromise attempted by the Union of Brest (Brześć) in 1596 failed to persuade the Orthodox peasant masses to accept Papal supremacy while maintaining their traditional liturgy in a Uniate or Greek Orthodox church. The Vazas promoted the Counter-Reformation and patronised the Jesuits. The Commonwealth gradually lost its dynamism during the seventeenth century as political and economic life decayed. Culture degenerated into self-satisfied *Sarmatianism*. Religious toleration was replaced by a fanaticism, fanned by the Counter-Reformation, which rendered the political compromises necessary for maintaining the heterogeneous Commonwealth impossible. These domestic factors, including the increasing use of the *liberum veto* after 1652, which allowed a single deputy to paralyse the Sejm, inevitably led to international decline.

The country was weakened by Bohdan Chmielnicki's uprising of 1648–51 in the Ukraine and the Swedish onslaught of 1655–60 despite the valiant fight-back led by Stefan Czarniecki. Prussia was lost to Brandenburg in 1657, the Inflanty (southern Estonia and Latvia) soon afterwards while Smolensk and the eastern Ukraine went to a resurgent Russia by the Truce of Andruszowo in 1667.[9] Despite one final upsurge under King Jan I Sobieski (1674–96) the Poles, as usual, gained little diplomatic benefit from his defeat of the Turks at Vienna in 1683. On his death the country fell into the hands of two successive Saxon kings. Challenged by French and Swedish supported rivals they surrendered Poland's independence and became Russian clients.[10]

NATIONAL DOWNFALL AND PARTITION

Every subsequent generation of Poles has debated the reasons for the loss of national independence and drawn vastly differing conclusions depending on the circumstances and needs of their time. Some have stressed the selfishness of foreign rulers and of the landowning classes as opening the way to national decline. But for every negative national memory of anti-patriotic confederations supporting foreign powers, notably those of Radom in 1767 and Targowica in 1792, there is a positive one. The confederation of Bar in 1768, supported by the great Czartoryski, Potocki and Lubomirski magnate clans, was unable to prevent the First Partition of Poland by Russia, Prussia and Austria in 1772 but it stimulated a strong movement for national and civic regeneration.[11] Influenced by the American Revolution the modernisation of the Polish state and society culminated in the work of the Four Year Sejm (1788–1792). The progressive constitution of 3rd May 1791 become a powerful symbol of democracy and national sovereignty for Poles.

Poland's enemies, however, took advantage of the French Revolution to partition Poland off the map of Europe. The Russians and the Prussians shared the spoils in the Second Partition of 1793 while the Austrians joined in the Third Partition of 1795.[12] The military struggle against the Russians in 1794 led by Tadeusz Kościuszko proved unsuccessful but initial victories such as that of Racławice produced potent images of peasants winning the day with their scythes, a scene immortalised in one of Jan Matejko's great paintings. Long-lasting national myths supporting the cause of Polish independence were further developed by the Napoleonic experience.[13] The clash between the Romanticism of the time and post-1863 Positivism found its highest expression in the novel 'Ashes' (*Popioły*) by Stefan Żeromski which was turned into an enormously popular and much discussed film in the 1960s by Andrzej Wajda. Napoleon disappointed the Poles, despite the large numbers who flocked to fight in his 'Legions'[14] giving them merely a truncated and short-lived Duchy of Warsaw from 1807–1813. His personal, as well as political, cynicism also showed itself in his treatment of his Polish mistress, Maria Walewska.[15] The Idealist–Realist debate in Polish politics and intellectual life can be traced back to this time. Powerful unifying symbols also emerged such as the Polish national anthem, a stirring mazurka beginning with the lines 'Poland is not yet lost' (*Jeszcze Polska nie zginęła!*), written by Józef Wybicki in 1797 when serving in General Dąbrowski's legion in Italy.

It has often been pointed out that the key feature of the partition period was that the Polish nation not only survived but became culturally and socially stronger and more conscious despite the loss of independence.[16] The tendency for Poles to view their nation and their society as quite separate from the, often, foreign controlled state, as in the Second World War and Communist periods, is something that is only now being alleviated in the final stage of modernisation involving full sovereignty and democratisation after 1989. Fragmentation and subjection to three very different types of rule for over a century also resulted in differentiated experiences which have left their mark in differing regional mentalities.

The domestic autonomy which the Russian-controlled Congress Kingdom benefitted from after 1815 came to an end after the November 1830 uprising which was suppressed militarily in 1831.[17] Growing Russification and repression led to the growth of a large 'Emigration' movement, notably in Paris led by Prince Adam Jerzy Czartoryski at the Hotel Lambert. An ingrained political tradition developed which was to recur throughout the nineteenth century and after the Second World War. The cause of national independence was intimately linked with a flowering of Romanticism in music with Frederyk Chopin and the works of Adam Mickiewicz, Juliusz Słowacki, Zygmunt Krasiński and Cyprian Kamil Norwid, in literature and in history with Joachim Lelewel. Such writers developed powerful national myths which sustained patriots and which were inculcated in Polish children. The image of Poland as a Christ amongst Nations whose suffering would be rewarded with independence reinforced the older idea that Poland was the bulwark of European civilisation against eastern barbarism as well as the Catholic *antemurale*. This matrix of values developed into the Idealist tradition which glorified the 1830–31 and January 1863 uprisings as heroic insurrections which kept the national spirit alive.[18]

However, a Positivist reaction set in after the suppression of the 1863 uprising which developed 'Organic Work' attitudes designed to strengthen the Polish community economically and socially while waiting for international events to weaken the occupying powers.[19] The Kraków historical school led by the conservative Michał Bobrzyński, who became governor of Austrian controlled Galicia, crystallised this view; it stressed the responsibility of weak political institutions and social divisions and derided revolutionary enthusiasm in the so-called *Stańczyk's Portfolio*. The rival Warsaw school admired the heroic cult of insurrection and emphasised international and economic factors in extenuation of Poland's downfall. The occupied and divided Polish nation, facing heavy repression from its Russian and Prussian overlords also responded with exceptional cultural vitality as exemplified in the novels, plays and poetry of Henryk Sienkiewicz, Bolesław Prus, Stefan Żeromski, Władysław Reymont and Stanisław Wyspiański, the operas of Stanisław Moniuszko and the paintings of Jan Matejko and Aleksander

Gierymski. A great role was played by Polish women and the family as well as Roman Catholic parish priests in protecting the national language from forced Russification and Germanification and in educating children in its literary canon.[20]

The growing development of industry and capitalism, however, created new social conflicts. The socialist movement in Poland was thus from the outset divided by the National Question. The significance of revolutionary internationalists such as Ludwik Waryński, Róża Luksemburg, Julian March-lewski and Feliks Dzierżyński who formed the Social-Democracy of the Kingdom of Poland and Lithuania (SDKPiL) was magnified out of all proportion during communist rule; the dominant political tradition was that of the Polish Socialist Party (PPS), one of whose wings led by Józef Piłsudski became predominantly nationalist. Both movements contended with a pleth-ora of provincial, Christian-democratic and peasant parties, the latter pro-ducing the notable figure of Wincenty Witos. Ideologically the right was divided between various conservative and liberal movements and the National Democrats (ND) led by the outstanding political ideologist, Roman Dmowski.[21]

INDEPENDENCE AND DEMOCRACY IN INTERWAR POLAND

We have already noted that modern Poland has been dominated by a perma-nent debate about the country's destiny and that constant themes recur in interpreting the interplay between its domestic and foreign policies [Leslie 1980]. The argument between Dmowski, who favoured a Russian alliance to counter what he viewed as the more dangerous German threat, and the Rus-sophobic Piłsudski who initially aligned his Riflemen's Brigades (or Legions) alongside the Central Powers in 1914 was resolved by the totally unexpected collapse of both empires at the end of the First World War. Germany's defeat and the Bolshevik Revolution were thus key factors in the regaining of Polish independence in November 1918 as promised in the Thirteenth Point of President Woodrow Wilson's war-aims.

It is often forgotten that the interwar Second Republic had to struggle for the recognition of her borders until 1923.[22] The border with Germany in-volved Polish uprisings and League of Nations' plebiscites in Silesia and East Prussia. The southern border entailed a minor, but bitter, conflict over Cieszyn which was occupied by Czechoslovakia in 1920 but seized by the Poles after Munich. The military struggle for the eastern frontier was a build up to the Polish-Soviet War of Summer 1920.[23] Piłsudski's victory before Warsaw enabled Polish forces to extend the border, confirmed by the Treaty of Riga in March 1921, well beyond the current post-Second World War border which roughly corresponded to a line named after Lord Curzon, the British Foreign Secretary. This antagonised the Ukrainians and Belarusans and rendered Piłsudski's already archaic *Federalist* schemes inoperable.[24] More seriously, the East Slav minorities incorporated in Poland were subjected to Polonisation. Dmowski's integral nationalism was applied increasingly by Piłsudski's ruling camp. Finally, one should note that the dispute over Vilnius (Wilno) was only resolved by its camouflaged occupation by General Żeligowski and actual incorporation into Poland in 1923. The result was a closed or 'dead' frontier and no diplomatic relations with Lithuania until 1938.[25]

Interwar Poland thus became a very multinational state but not all the minorities were either contented or loyal to the Polish state as shown most notably in Ukrainian UNDO terrorism and pro-Nazi Fifth Column German activity in the 1930s. In 1931 a maximum 69% of the 32 million population were ethnic Poles while there were roughly 5 million Ukrainians, 3.1 million Jews, 1.9 million Belarusans, 800,000 Germans and 200,000 Lithuanians. The treatment of the Jewish community has raised particularly intense debate because of its terrible fate subsequently in the Holocaust. The issue is, however, extremely complicated because of both the varied Polish political and social policies and the equally diverse assimilationist, Zionist (return to Israel), Chassidic (religious fundamentalist) and leftist-secular (communist, socialist and Bundist) reactions within the Jewish community.[26]

Although, and perhaps because, Piłsudski was Head of State from 1918 to 1922 the idea of a strong presidency was eventually rejected in favour of an assembly-system in which parliament dominated until 1926. After the assassination of the first president, Gabriel Narutowicz, by a rightwing fanatic in late 1922, Poland was ruled by weak and shortlived coalition governments. But the conflicts between Piłsudski and his ND and Peasant Party opponents in the Sejm, especially over the control of the armed forces, escalated into his armed seizure of power in May 1926, involving some 300 deaths. President Stanisław Wojciechowski was replaced by Piłsudski's nominee, Ignacy Mościcki, who remained in office until 1939. The constitution was amended to allow Piłsudski to rule Poland from behind the scenes through his political nominees and his control of the army while the liberal 1921 constitution was replaced by an authoritarian one in 1935. A relatively liberal phase from 1926–1930 was followed by repression until Piłsudski's death in May 1935 when political opponents were interned, tried or forced into exile. His *Sanacja* (Moral Reform) movement was converted into a Camp of National Unity (OZON) by his successors, a *troika* consisting of President Mościcki, Marshal Śmigły-Rydz, the new Inspector-General of the Armed Forces, and

Foreign Minister Józef Beck. Poland's interwar political system, oscillating between an extreme form of parliamentary democracy and limited, if growing, authoritarianism, thus hardly provides an entirely convincing model for post-1989 democrats.

Poland's external security in the 1920s was assured by Western alliances notably the 1921 alliance and military convention with France. But the 1925 Locarno agreement showed that Poland's interests would not be guaranteed in any great power understanding. The League of Nations was also too weak to enforce its high ideals of collective security. With the rise of Nazi Germany and the re-emergence of Soviet Russia in the early 1930s Poland not only faced growing threats from more powerful, ideologically hostile and revisionist neighbours but also the danger of their rapprochment at her expense which had already been demonstrated by their 1922 Rapallo agreement. The above analysis led Piłsudski to appoint a new foreign minister, Józef Beck, in 1932 who remained paramount in this sphere until 1939. Beck attempted to balance by signing non-aggression pacts with the USSR in 1932 and Germany in 1934 and distanced himself from a weakened France and a disinterested Britain.[27] He should not be blamed for the latter's failure to react to Hitler's remilitarisation of the Rhineland in 1936, the *Anschluss* of Austria and the Munich surrender in 1938; but Western public opinion was hostile to Poland's domestic authoritarianism, illiberal treatment of national minorities and attempts to balance between hostile great powers in Eastern Europe.[28] All this has had an unfavourable effect on the country's subsequent historical reputation. The interwar republic re-united the country and achieved some, albeit uneven, success in social and economic modernisation. The failure to maintain democracy and independence or to complete economic and rural transformation should not be judged too harshly, given the East European conditions of the time; but it provides a partial explanation for the initial support for major, if not revolutionary, social and economic change after the Second World War.

THE SECOND WORLD WAR

Although Britain guaranteed Poland against aggression after Hitler's occupation of Bohemia and Moravia in March 1939 little could, or was, done to prepare for its military implementation nor were any additional teeth given to the Franco–Polish alliance. Historians have debated whether the Western Powers were at fault in not making sufficient counter-offers to prevent the USSR from signing the Ribbentrop-Molotov pact of 23 August 1939.[29] But Hitler's demands on the Poles to cede Danzig and the extra-territorial road across the Polish Corridor to East Prussia were merely the symbolic form for accepting satellite status within the Anti-Comintern Pact. Beck voiced the Piłsudski camp's tradition of national honour and independence by rejecting submission out of hand. He hoped that the Western alliance would deter Hitler but he should be accused of no more than tactical inflexibility. Poland had no way of resolving her 'two enemies' dilemma given Western weakness and the brutal *realpolitik* of the time. Should outsiders really blame her for refusing to chose voluntarily between German Nazism and Soviet Communism?

The catastrophic results for Poland was that her badly led, poorly equipped and awkwardly positioned armed forces, despite fighting bravely were smashed in the German *blitzkrieg* of September.[30] The country succumbed to the Fourth Partition when the USSR occupied eastern Poland after 17 September on the basis of the secret protocol of the German-Soviet pact and incorporated it in the Ukrainian and Belarusan republics.[31] The Germans annexed part of their occupied territory to the Reich and also established a brutal and unbridled reign of terror in the remaining General-Government.[32]

It is difficult to exaggerate the physical and psychological consequences of the Second World War on Poland.[33] About six million Poles including an estimated three million Jews lost their lives, about 40% of the economy, 70% of the transport infrastucture and large numbers of cities and buildings were destroyed. Along with the Ukraine, Belarus and Bosnia, Poland undoubtedly suffered the greatest human and physical losses of any country during the War. The Nazis established a network of extermination camps, of which Auschwitz, Majdanek, Treblinka and Sobibór were the largest, and carried out a merciless and efficient Holocaust of Jews and gypsies.[34] Vast numbers of Poles were deported to work as slave labourers in Germany or dispersed into the depths of Asiatic or Siberian Russia. About 14,700 Polish officers captured by the Soviets in the September campaign were taken from three camps and murdered by the NKVD in Summer 1940 in the atrocity that bears the generic name of Katyń.[35] Hundreds of thousands found their way to the West and never returned, forming yet another 'Emigration'. Finally, the dreadful wartime experience of arbitrary street-round-ups, shootings and public executions as well as continual humiliation and danger strengthened and re-legitimated the state-society split. Social and economic habits of opposition and disengagement continued as negative features throughout the communist period and after.

There is insufficient space here to follow the Polish Question during the Second World War.[36] What one can say is that the Western Allies gave no more than ambiguous and equivocal support to the Polish government-in-exile led by General Władysław Sikorski until his death in a faulty Liberator bomber off Gibraltar in July 1943.[37] Polish troops under General Władysław Anders fought in the North African and Italian campaigns, covering themselves in glory, particularly, at Monte Cassino in January–May 1944. The Poles also organised the Home Army (AK) within Poland, loyal to the London government, the largest resistance movement in occupied Europe.[38] But the Nazi attack on the USSR in 1941 meant that the Allies initially gave priority to supporting the Soviet war-effort. After the tide turned at Stalingrad they were in an increasingly weak position to protect Polish interests. Large numbers of Poles deported from Soviet-occupied areas were allowed to leave the USSR through Persia in 1942. The Soviets set up the the the so-called Berling Army, after its first commander, out of the remainder to fight on the Eastern Front. The lie of German responsibility for Katyń was, however, maintained in order not to offend Stalin. Now that the dust has settled one can also note the despicable fact that the pretence was continued officially by some Western governments until after the fall of Soviet communism.

Once the Soviets had smashed the Nazi war-machine and entered Poland from Summer 1944 onwards, the allied bargaining position became ever more dependent on Soviet goodwill. Sikorski's successors, the more conciliatory, peasant party (PSL) leader Stanisław Mikołajczyk and, the intransigeant, PPS chairman, Tomasz Arciszewski, were both impaled on the other, Soviet Communism, fork of Poland's 'two enemies' dilemma. The last independent Polish attempt to change the course of history in the grand Idealist manner was the Warsaw Uprising of August to September 1944. The whole city rose up in the heroic tradition of the nineteenth century insurrections and fought overwhelmingly superior German military forces for 63 days.[39] The London Poles can be criticised for naiveté in hoping that Stalin would support their 'Tempest' (*Burza*) strategy of seizing control of the capital in order to strengthen their political position;[40] the national AK leadership also probably mistimed Red Army capacity to help as Rokossowky's offensive had petered out and was genuinely unable to renew itself until Warsaw's eventual liberation in January 1945. But, as in 1939, the Poles had no political or psychological alternative except for a Czech form of submission to overwhelming odds which ran against the national character of the exiled and resistance Poles.

Stalin had already made it clear that he viewed the AK as a national and class enemy by arresting its officers who had earlier come out of *konspiracja* to contact the Red Army. He established a Polish Committee of National Liberation (PKWN) in Chełm on 22nd July 1944 which turned into the Lublin government on 1st January 1945. These entirely Soviet sponsored and controlled forces benefitted from the failure of the uprising and the Nazi reprisals which destroyed over 90% of Warsaw's buildings, resulting in around 200,000 deaths and the expulsion and dispersion of its population. A whole generation consequently swung back towards attitudes of political realism which dominated until the 1970s. The hopeless dilemma of not just the nationalist, conservative and anti-Soviet Poles but of all those who had hoped that an independent Poland would emerge at the end of the Second World War was depicted most poignantly in Jerzy Andrzejewski's novel, *Ashes and Diamonds*, and in Wajda's powerful film of the same name.

The London Poles considered that they were 'sold-out' to Stalin by the Western allies at the end of the Second World War. They divided, though, as Mikołajczyk's realist wing considered that this was inevitable and attempted to make the best of it. The Yalta Agreement of February 1945 accepted Stalin's 1939 annexation of Poland's prewar Eastern Territories and set a border corresponding closely to the Curzon Line. Poland was compensated by being shifted westwards. She was awarded most of East Prussia as well as the 'Recovered' or Western Territories up to the old Piast frontier of a thousand years earlier on the line of the rivers Oder and the Lusatian Neisse (Nysa). The Provisional Lublin government was widened to include Mikołajczyk and some London Poles in what was initially a genuine coalition.[41] This was clearly dominated from the outset by the newly established communist party, the Polish Workers' Party (PPR) led by its First Secretary, Władysław Gomułka, and Bolesław Bierut the chairman of the National Council of the Homeland (KRN). The central issue at Yalta, however, was the commitment to the holding of free-elections in Poland which the democratic forces were expected to win. President Roosevelt hoped that Stalin would concede this in exchange for Western agreement to the new frontiers and the guaranteeing of Soviet security interests in the region through the Red Army presence especially in the new Soviet zone of defeated and divided Germany. In the event such free elections were not to take place in Poland for over four decades. The hoped-for Finnish model was not applied in Eastern Europe for all the wider reasons which led to the ideological, political and military division of Europe, the establishment of the Iron Curtain and the development of the Cold War and of an increasingly restrictive form of Soviet control and Stalinist communism in the region.

Although it is currently unfashionable, as the communists misused the factor for their propaganda purposes, one needs to reiterate the scale and intensity of the changes brought about by the Second World War. Poland's territory shrunk by 23% to its current area of 312,700 square kilometres.

Vast population transfers coupled with the 6 million deaths transformed the population out of all recognition. The problem of national minorities was resolved by the deportation and relocation of 1.5 million ethnic Poles from the Eastern Territories and the departure of most of the Germans along with over half a million Ukrainians, Belarusans and Lithuanians. The bulk of the residual Jewish community, decimated by the Nazis, either left for Israel in the late-1940s (about 140,000) or subsequently, especially during the Partisan purge of 1967–68 (about 12,000). Vast numbers of Poles remained in the USSR until the late 1950s or in 'emigration', especially in Western Europe animating important centres of opposition to communist rule, notably the Paris based monthly *Kultura*. The result was that Poland assumed its current ethnically homogeneous and Roman Catholic character. Modernisation has thus been facilitated in this one important respect.

PEOPLE'S POLAND: FROM STALINIST SATELLITE TO NATIONAL DOMESTICISM

The first stage of communist rule in Poland was its transformation into a monopoly system by 1948. Opposition was worn down and gradually eliminated. The referendum issues of the western frontier, nationalisation and land reform in June 1946 were uncontroversial but the opposition made a symbolic stand over the abolition of the Senate. We now know that the results were rigged and that communist claims of 68% support were untrue.[42] Even greater intimidation and falsification took place in the January 1947 election where the PPR led alliance gained 394 out of 444 Sejm seats with an alleged 80% of the vote.[43] Growing repression forced Mikołajczyk to flee the country. The communists split the democratic, peasant and socialist parties. The former two survived during the communist era as minor parties called the Democratic (SD) and United Peasant (ZSL) parties. They were given representation in the Sejm and local councils. Although they were rigidly controlled during Stalinism they were allowed, after 1956, to act as limited pressure groups. The collaborating PPS wing was incorporated into a new Polish United Workers Party (PZPR) in December 1948. Its leader, the cunning Józef Cyrankiewicz, was prime minister for most of the period up till 1970. Other ex-socialists such as foreign minister Adam Rapacki maintained distinctive slants which contributed to the pluralist Polish model.

This brings us to the central issue of the degree of support for the establishment of communist power in what officially became the Polish People's Republic (PRL) with the new constitution of 1952. What is often forgotten today is the extent to which the weak and peripheral form of Polish capitalism had been discredited by its failure to resolve the problems of the two thirds of the interwar population who lived, and often vegetated as 'surplus population' in the countryside. The excesses of foreign capitalism also did not offer, at that time, an attractive or feasible model for Poland's industrialisation and modernisation. Parliamentary democracy had not consolidated itself while Piłsudski's model of guided democracy and limited authoritarianism was equally contested. Second World War brutalisation of attitudes and behaviour strengthened the case for a radical, if not socialist, transformation of the Polish economy and society. It is unpopular and controversial to say this today, but there was general support for the state's role in the rebuilding of a new secular and more egalitarian, Poland; but it is also true that most Poles found it very difficult to reconcile this aspiration with Soviet control, let alone its extreme post-1948 Stalinist form.

There has been a long-standing debate, both political and academic, about the apportionment of blame for Poland's crises and relative backwardness since 1945. Some like Leszek Moczulski, the national independence camp leader, have blamed Soviet Russian control and Poland's limited sovereignty within the Warsaw Pact in a root and branch way for all the country's ills. Many Western political scientists and domestic dissidents also argued that communism was unreformable. Its essentially totalitarian character implied monopoly control which ruled out political pluralism and democratisation and made it very difficult to introduce market reforms into the command economy although Yugoslavia and Hungary had done so.[44] The contrary comparative case was that post-1956 Poland was at the liberal and nationalist end of the communist studies spectrum. The empirical evidence was that the PZPR had adjusted to living with social and cultural pluralism and had adopted the everyday framework of national Polish values.[45] Repeated conflicts in 1956, 1968, 1970 and 1980–81 supported the argument that the traditional state-society rift kept renewing itself in new forms. The final peaceful and negotiated collapse of communism in 1989 confirmed Zbigniew Brzezinski's argument; Poland was the best example of communist Systemic Failure being aggravated by Organic Rejection due to cultural factors causing a long process of internal transformation.[46]

The PZPR under Władysław Gomułka (First Secretary, October 1956-December 1970) and even more so under his successor until September 1980, Edward Gierek, wrested a substantial form of domestic autonomy. It is true that they reiterated the primacy of Marxist–Leninist ideology and of the Soviet alliance and continually disappointed reformers. In practice, however, the PZPR had to balance between Polish society and Soviet pressures for maintaining uniformity and cohesion within their *bloc*. The result was that the PZPR kept up what increasingly proved to be the shallow fiction of its leading-role. In order to do so it had to resort to repeated concessions and grant various degrees of autonomy to social groups such as the peasantry and intellectuals in 1956, the workers in 1980 and most notably the Roman Catholic church. It had to apply ideologically unorthodox and creative political responses ranging from Gomułka's domesticism, Moczar's national communism in1968, Gierek's consumerism and Jaruzelski's technocratic and pluralist authoritarianism in order to survive. Towards the end of its life the PZPR even considered Eurocommunist arguments, presented in the 'Kubiak Report' of 1983.[47] The source of all political and social crises, according to the latter, had lain with the incomplete and delayed reform of the Stalinist structures and mechanisms of party-rule established at the outset. All this seemed to confirm the post-1989 argument that full modernisation was only possible through bourgeois-liberal democratisation, marketisation and re-integration into the European and world capitalist framework.

The academic and value-free history of communist or People's Poland still remains to be written for all the contentious reasons of political commitment and conflict which have been indicated above, although there is a vast literature on specific events and sub-periods.[48] The reader might, however, bear the following signposts to its evolution in mind as a preamble to the post-1989 development of democratic Poland.

1) The Stalinisation period was short-lived from roughly 1948 to 1955.[49] Its main feature, rapid and wholesale industrialisation on the basis of the command economy planning system, was put in place by Hilary Minc. The collectivisation of agriculture was initiated, but at a very slow rate. The third classic feature, mass terror, also did not assume 1930s Soviet or contemporary Hungarian proportions. Gomułka's disgrace and the purge of his supporters, who had spent the war in the communist resistance in Poland, involved recantation of their line on the country's national peculiarities in building socialism but not physical elimination. The so-called *Muscovites* led by president Bierut did not organise show-trials and were content with limiting the purge to the military and security areas. Having said that, a Soviet Marshal, Konstanty Rokossowski (in the Polish form), became minister of defence, a prominent PZPR politburo member, Jakub Berman, ran the security services on Stalinist lines while Minc set up the bureaucracy of Five Year Plans and subordinated the Polish economy to the Soviet and Comecon framework.

Stalin's death in March 1953 and subsequent de-Stalinisation meant that the attempt to build a totalitarian system in Poland was shortlived and incomplete. It led to a crisis that caused it to be abandoned in 1956. The Stalinist secret police (UB) were brought under party control in 1954–55 while intellectuals such as the poet Adam Ważyk in his *Poem for Adults* expressed social discontent. Political decompression led to the PZPR leadership splitting into two factions, especially after Bierut's death in Moscow in March 1956. The Natolin faction, backed by Rokossowski, attempted to save full Soviet control and neo-Stalinism by demagogic concessions to the workers and such ploys as anti-semiticism. Its opponents, the Puławy faction wanted domestic reforms to modify Stalinism and a re-adjustment of Soviet links as promised in Khruschev's February 1956 'Secret Speech'. The resulting power-struggle paralysed the PZPR's monopoly. Intellectual and political debate developed and workers' discontent with Stalinist austerity took organised form and burst out in the Poznań Uprising of late June which caused 75 deaths. All this built up to the great crisis of October 1956 which was resolved by Gomułka's return to power against Soviet opposition and threats of military invasion.[50]

2) Gomułka was the symbol of *October* because he had stood up to the Stalinists in 1948 but the deal between the communist state and Polish society was ambiguous and wrongly understood by the latter leading to subsequent disenchantment. What occurred was that the Stalinisation, especially the collectivisation, drive was abandoned as was the campaign against the Roman Catholic church whose primate, Cardinal Stefan Wyszyński, in return called on Poles to support the new regime in the Sejm elections of January 1957. Intellectual, cultural and social life benefitted from less party control while contacts with the West became more open. But Gomułka was a very orthodox communist who maintained the primacy of the heavy industrialisation drive and the dogmas of the PZPR's leading-role and the Soviet alliance. Within a year he brought back hardliners into leading positions and denounced reformers who wanted to go structurally beyond *October* as revisionists. He defined the Polish road to communism in terms of domestic autonomy. His brand of communist leadership took the country's national, Catholic, intellectual and peasant landowning peculiarities into account in building socialism and generally eschewed mass mobilisation and repression except within the crucial party and industrial sectors.

The result was an odd hybrid, which looked promising in 1956 when state and society came together for a short heady moment, but which was left behind by Khruschev's second de-Stalinisation wave in 1961.[51] The stagnation of the 'Small Stabilisation' was marked by continual conflicts between the regime, intellectuals and the Catholic church notably in 1966 over whether Poland's Millenium was celebrating a thousand years of statehood or Catholicism. Impressive achievements were recorded in rebuilding the country and its infrastructure and vast industrial plants mushroomed but the price of enormous investment rates was social poverty. Little time or funding was devoted to raising the standard of living. The result was another great political and social crisis, triggered by an intra-party national-ist authoritarian challenge to Gomułka which simmered until workers' strikes in the Baltic seacoast region brought Gomułka down in December 1970.

A Partisan faction, led by minister of the interior, Mieczysław Moczar, initiated an 'Anti-Zionist' purge of the PZPR after the Arab-Israeli war of 1967.[52] The student and artistic milieux were provoked, by the banning of a patriotic play by Mickiewicz, into sit-ins and demonstrations which were brutally repressed in March 1968.[53] The main aim of the exercise was a Soviet-supported drive to cow Polish society and to purge individuals from the party who might have been minded to copy the ongoing Prague Spring. This became clearly apparent when Gomułka participated enthus-iastically in the Warsaw Pact invasion of Czechoslovakia in August 1968; in return for which service he was endorsed again as PZPR first Secretary by Brezhnev. But although intellectuals and reformers were disciplined, the working class explosion was only postponed. The signing of the Polish-German treaty normalising their relations by confirming the Oder-Neisse frontier in December 1970 removed one of the main arguments justifying Poland's dependence upon the USSR. An important psychological change was to develop consequently during the 1970s. The immediate spark in December 1970 was, however, a large increase in the price of food, espe-cially meat, which was, paradoxically, necessitated by a proposed economic reform involving financial restructuring.

3) It was originally thought that the loss of at least 45 lives caused by the intervention of armed troops and tanks in Gdańsk, Gdynia and Szczecin had been caused primarily by incompetence and conflicting lines of responsibility but recently published documents suggest more direct culpability.[54] Edward Gierek (born 1913), who replaced Gomułka as PZPR First Secretary had been a highly successful and popular provincial chieftain in Silesia and repre-sented the party's industrial-managerial lobby. Gierek was forced by contin-uing strikes in the Baltic shipyards and Łódź to rescind the price increase but most importantly to engage in direct dialogue with the workers. He pro-mised the resolution of future disputes on a negotiated basis eschewing the use of force. For a while during 1971 he considered reforms, particularly economic ones. But the bloc-wide reassertion of communist *apparats* under Brezhnev after the suppression of the Prague Spring yet again ruled out the necessary structural reforms. Even without these reforms Gierek's Poland changed fundamentally in an informal way during his decade of rule into a

more open and modern society. The stresses of transformation and the lack of political mechanisms for resolving social crises, however, led not only to his own downfall but also, after some delay, to the ultimate fall of the communist system itself. His policy of consumerism based on a high degree of borrowing from the West produced a boom in the first half of the decade with more flats, food and consumer goods becoming available. But higher interest rates and the hard currency deficit of $20 billion by 1980 brought his dash for growth to a spectacular close with GDP actually declining in 1978–81. Mammoth prestige industrial projects like the Huta Katowice steelworks were also only partially completed adding to the drain on resources. At the end of the day Gierek's policy of technological modernisation and of export-led growth proved a premature pipe-dream.[55]

But one should remember that a better educated generation with higher expectations and without the restraining memories of the Second World War and Stalinist hardships came onto the political scene in the 1970s. Gierek partly catered to the burgeoning university educated professional classes by providing a less ideological, more pragmatic and more meritocratic PZPR whose membership expanded to 3 million at its peak in 1980. But initial concessions to the peasantry were followed by mismanagement of the rural sector leading to food and meat shortages. Industrial workers also lost ground relative to other social groups. Foremen and supervisers as well as slightly better skilled and, what an expressive Polish term describes as, quarter-educated (ćwierćinteligent) workers of the Wałęsa-type felt that the system was discriminating against them. They grew alienated from the party bureaucracy in the factories. This more demanding generation was also not limited by the sense of external threat. Gierek completed Poland's opening up to the outside world by normalising relations with the Vatican and the Roman Catholic church and by contributing in full to the more relaxed East–West detente.

Gierek had a major falling out with the intellectuals and professionals in 1975–76 over proposed amendments to the constitution which would have formalised party-rule and enshrined brotherly links with the USSR as the basis of its foreign relations. But the real challenge came from the workers who again prevented Gierek's initial attempt to reassert financial rationality by raising food-prices in June 1976. An immediate national strike led to their rescinding within a day; but Gierek then resorted to traditional communist repressive and propaganda methods in suppressing riots and demonstrations in Radom, Płock and at the Ursus tractor factory. The result was the organisation of open opposition in the form of the Workers Defense Committee (KOR) with Jacek Kuroń (born 1934) and Adam Michnik (born 1946) as its main leaders and of Leszek Moczulski's (born 1930) national independence movement in 1978.[56]

Gierek underestimated the extent of Poland's economic and political problems and failed to respond sufficiently strongly until February 1980 when he sacked his long-time prime minister Piotr Jaroszewicz. But traditional organisational-directive methods of party-rule proved unavailing.[57] Dissidents argued that consultative and negotiated methods should be applied in order to gain society's support for austerity and restructuring measures. Part of the price should also be paid by the party elite which had become corrupt and materialist and whose incompetence and privileges had provoked the crisis. No-one should, therefore, have been surprised when another attempted price-rise in Summer 1980 not only provoked a crisis leading to leadership and regime change but also came closer to achieving systemic transformation than in 1956.

4) What was wholly unforeseen was the extent to which the workers and their intellectual advisers learnt political and organisational lessons from the 1970 experience. The sit-in or occupation strike, most notably in the Gdańsk and Szczecin shipyards following a long-drawn out wave of strikes and pro-tests against the price-increase all over Poland, forced the authorities into direct negotiations. Equally important, once the crucial shift from purely economic to political demands took place in Gdańsk in the third week of August the organisation of Inter-factory Strike Committees (MKS) provided a defence against workplaces being picked-off individually. Deputy-prime minister Mieczysław Jagielski was, therefore, forced to concede the crucial rights to strike and to organise free trade-unions in the most important Gdańsk Agreement of 31 August which along with those of Szczecin and Jas-trzębie are referred to as the 1980 Social Agreements.[58] The Independent and Self-Managing Trade-Union (NSZZ) Solidarity then emerged out of regional MKSs during September; it was joined by over 80% of the work-force in a dramatic outflow from the official communist trade unions. The communist state thus retreated and accepted political and trade union plural-ism and a fundamental limitation of its leading-role. Gierek was replaced as First Secretary by a pragmatic and cautious party *apparatchik*, Stanisław Kania (born 1927), who was preferred to Gierek's more nationalist rival, Ste-fan Olszowski (born 1931).

The key question was whether the PZPR genuinely accepted the August 1980 agreements or whether it had merely been forced into a tactical retreat in order to gain time to regroup. Most commentators favour the latter view but they also underestimate the priority which the USSR gave to preventing the PZPR leadership from falling into reformist hands willing to work with

Solidarity and the new realities and the internal pressure which they applied in order to achieve this end. The most serious threat of Soviet military invasion occurred just before the December 1980 Central Committee plenum in order to prevent reformist leaders like Tadeusz Fiszbach (born 1935), the Gdańsk province PZPR First Secretary, from coming to the fore. Kania's centrist leadership worked out a form of co-existence with Solidarity despite continuing confrontations over its registration which postponed the issue of the PZPR's leading-role.

Numerous local and social explosions were mediated by the Roman Catholic church and by Solidarity's intellectual advisers, notably Kuroń. But Kania rallied the residual PZPR hard-core or *aktyw* while an increasingly important role was played by the Army commander, the minister of defence, General Wojciech Jaruzelski (born 1923), who became prime minister in February 1981. He conciliated, at first, through his deputy-prime minister, Mieczysław Rakowski (born 1926), the long-time reforming editor of the influential Warsaw weekly, *Polityka*. Rakowski negotiated the legitimation of Rural Solidarity and helped to smooth-over the major crisis caused by the beating-up of three Solidarity activitists in Bydgoszcz in March 1981. The PZPR then renewed its ideological legitimacy in its own strictly Marxist-Leninist terms. It carried out a controlled democratisation process involving the election of delegates to its Ninth Congress, the voting-in of a largely new top leadership and the condemnation of Gierek's mistakes in July 1981. The key factor, again, was that the party-reformers notably grassroots Horizantalists, as well as the more extreme hardliners of the *Grunwald* type were outmanoeuvred. The Kania-Jaruzelski domesticist leadership thus retained control of the PZPR but the rejection of Eurocommunist policies also effectively ruled out the possibility of a deal with Solidarity.[59] When Jaruzelski replaced Kania as First Secretary in October the imposition of martial law, despite Soviet displeasure at its continual postponement, merely became a question of timing.[60]

Communist relations with Solidarity had been marked by continual conflict, both at the national and local levels but these were kept largely in check. By early August 1981, when Rakowski entered into negotiations with the Solidarity leadership, society was demoralised and demobilised by the economic situation and consumer shortages which had reached rock-bottom. His failure to offer concessions or any acceptable basis for a domestic pact was both crucial and indicative. On the other hand Solidarity was also divided in its political responses. Wałęsa was criticised for his erratic and authoritarian leadership; perceptive commentators doubted whether Dual Power between Solidarity and the communists could continue without either a basic confrontation or a negotiated clarification of its parameters. The doctrine that Solidarity was 'Self-Limiting' became a popular catchword but it is doubtful if it had any alternative.[61] Solidarity went on to hold an 18-day congress in two rounds in September–October but its debates failed to crystallise a basis for political compromise.[62] The event had great moral and psychological significance in ensuring the long-term survival of Solidarity's values throughout the repression of the 1980s and in boosting the growth of a civil society.[63] Subsequent Solidarity demands for a referendum on self-management certainly did not precipitate the declaration of martial law on 13 December.

The Polish communist leadership, both for reasons of its own domestic power and of the limits set by a very conservative Brezhnev leadership, was determined to force its own solution to the political crisis upon Solidarity and Polish society.[64] The most they would concede in their version of a Historic Compromise was that Solidarity and its supporters should now enter a corporatist Front of National Understanding, thus accepting the PZPR's leading-role.[65] This Solidarity had refused to do from the outset in Autumn 1980. The consequence of this incorporation would, however, have been an even greater and fundamental revision of the communist system in a pluralist direction than had occurred in 1956. This would have provided the political basis for forcing an initially painful, although essential, economic reform on society. Such ideas were to resurface in the late 1980s, but as in 1981, were to be defeated by the realities of the East–West ideological-systemic conflict and by the hardliners in both camps.

5) The initial repression of martial life, although dramatic, was very efficiently carried out with relatively little loss of life or open resistance apart from in a few coalmines. Solidarity's leadership and hard-core was rounded-up and interned. Army officers replaced the party *apparat* in the new ruling Military Council of National Salvation (WRON) led by Jaruzelski. But the resort to force and the abandonment of negotiation and compromise divided a generation of Poles irrevocably, even though it did not signify the return to Stalinism. The historical and cultural values favouring the emergence of a counter-society continued into the early 1980s. An extensive Solidarity underground with vast publishing and social activities emerged which organised periodic street confrontations with the armed police (ZOMO). It proved that Solidarity, depite de-legalisation in September 1982, could not be extirpated even though it was much weakened.

On the other hand the formal ending of martial law in July 1983 did not signify a return to normality and orthodox methods of PZPR party rule.[66] Some generals like Jaruzelski himself and the crafty minister of the interior, Czesław Kiszczak (born 1925), continued in prominent positions. Party membership and morale as well as the *aktyw's* social implanation in workplaces and other institutions never recovered. New bodies such as the Patriotic Front for National Renewal (PRON), the OPZZ trade union movement and Jaruzelski's Consultative Council were established but only enjoyed qualified support.[67] The favourite words to describe the early to middle 1980s were, therefore, stalemate, deadlock and log-jam. It was clear that while the Army had saved the communist system, the latter was far from regaining more than a degree of control over society, and only achieved a moderate degree of legitimacy and support. On the other hand financial stabilisation in 1982 led to limited economic recovery. There was much talk of economic reform, especially during 1985–88 when Zbigniew Messner was prime minister, linked to attempts to gain social support through new consultative bodies. Jaruzelski's mixed model of consultative and technocratic authoritarianism seemed to have some chance of implanting itself for a moment in the mid-1980s.[68] Gorbachev's accession to power in Moscow initially encouraged reformism but then, fatally, undermined the long-term capacity for consolidating a new compromise system.[69]

Many of the underlying reasons for the collapse of communism in Poland have already been touched on in the preceding historical overview. The final stages are still controversial. The Second Solidarity, which re-emerged into the open in 1988, especially in Lech Wałęsa's Civic Comittee of December, was initially a very elitist body compared to the mass-based First Solidarity of 1980–81. Its claim that Solidarity organised the strikes of Spring-Summer 1988, following food price-rises, which started the train of events leading to the transfer of power is, in addition, very dubious. The truth is that the authorities interpreted workers' discontent as having peaked. The PZPR Central Committee's August 1988 plenum, therefore, decided that it was a favourable moment to renew negotiations with the opposition for its much sought after Anti-Crisis Pact to establish a political coalition which would gain social support for the Economic Reform. It had already failed to achieve this decisively on its own in the 1987 referendum when it had only gained 46% approval. The preliminary talks headed by Kiszczak bogged down in the Autumn over the issues of personalities, the agenda and the extent and means of Solidarity's re-legalisation. Following Rakowski's appointment as prime minister the political deadlock had to be unblocked by a heavily choreographed confrontation between Jaruzelski's reformers and the residual hardliners at the PZPR's January 1989 plenum. The way thus opened up for the Round Table talks of March-April and the agreement on the holding of the June elections. This eventually led to the wholly peaceful takeover of power by a Solidarity coalition Government headed by Tadeusz Mazowiecki (born 1927) in August which will be examined in greater detail in the next chapter.[70]

INQUEST ON COMMUNIST POLAND

Political scientists have argued that systemic petrification occurred in Poland because the political instutions and mechanisms of communist party mono-poly rule always lagged behind social demands, economic modernisation and cultural expectations [Kolankiewicz & Lewis 1988]. The resultant conflicts between state and society, according to Ray Taras, caused the six major con-frontations, discussed in this chapter, before the final collapse [Taras 1986]. Jacek Kuroń also concedes that the system responded and changed step by step from 1954 onwards as a result of these pressures; hardly surprisingly, he also claims the credit for its ultimate democratisation for the opposition forces in which he had played such a prominent role.[71] The vigorous debate in post-1989 Poland on the communist experience has, therefore, continued to reflect the political interests and values of the various parties and camps jockey-ing for power. For example, a high-powered series of articles in the weekly *Tygodnik Powszechny* in 1994–95 demonstrated the post-Solidarity and lib-eral camp's fear of gradual re-communization occasioned by the left's victory in the 1993 Sejm elections.[72] Sociologists like Janine Wedel had always been aware of the complexity of life under socialism and of the importance of informal mechanisms in resolving social and economic tensions.[73] Others like Mira Marody tended to blame that experience for many post-communist individual and social pathologies.[74] The one feature on which there has been general agreement is that the *Polish Paradoxes* caused by underlying cultural and historical traditions, have continued as powerful forces into the post-communist period [Gomułka & Polonsky 1990].

1   Direct reference to the enormous Polish language literature has generally been avoided in this chap-ter although the reader is referred to the bibliography as well as to the volumes which follow for informational purposes. For a guide see George Sanford & Adriana Gozdecka-Sanford, *Poland. World Bibliographical Series Volume 32* (Oxford: Clio Press, 1993). On the other hand the vener-able *Cambridge History of Poland* edited by William F. Reddaway (Cambridge: Cambridge UP, 2 Vols, 1941 & 1950) badly needs up-dating. It might also be useful to refer to *Atlas Historyczny Polski* (Warsaw: PPWK, 1973) for Poland's changing historical boundaries.

2   Joanna Hanson, *The Civilian Population and the Warsaw Uprising of 1944* (Cambridge: Cambridge UP, 1982).

3   Norman Davies, *Europe: A History* (Oxford: OUP, 1996).

4 Witold Hensel, *The Beginnings of the Polish State* (Warsaw: PWN, 1960). Tadeusz Manteuffel, *The Formation of the Polish State: The Period of Ducal Rule, 963–1194* (Detroit: Wayne State UP, 1990).

5 Paul Knoll, *The Rise of the Polish Monarchy: Piast Poland in East Central Europe, 1320–1370* (Chicago: Chicago UP, 1970).

6 Paweł Jasienica, *Piast Poland* (New York: Hippocrene, 1985).

7 William J. Rose, *Poland* (Harmondsworth: Penguin, 1939), p. 26.

8 Harry E. Dembinski, *The Union of Lublin in the Golden Age* (New York: Columbia UP, 1982). Paweł Jasienica, *The Commonwealth of Both Nations (Poland and Lithuania. The Silver Age* (New York: Hippocrene, 1987).

9 Martyn Rady, *The Tsars, Russia, Poland and the Ukraine, 1462–1725* (London: Hodder & Stoughton, 1990).

10 Jerzy T. Lukowski, *Liberty's Folly. The Polish-Lithuanian Commonwealth in the Eighteenth Century* (London: Routledge, 1991).

11 Herbert H. Kaplan, *The First Partition of Poland* (New York: Columbia UP, 1962).

12 Robert H. Lord, *The Second Partition of Poland* (Cambridge Mass: Harvard UP, 1915).

13 Andrzej Walicki, *The Enlightenment and the Birth of Modern Nationhood: Polish Political Thought from Noble Republicanism to Tadeusz Kościuszko* (Notre Dame Ind: University of Notre Dame Press, 1989).

14 Francis L. Petre, *Napoleon's Campaign in Poland, 1806–7* (London: Greenhill, 1989).

15 Christine Sutherland, *Marie Walewska: Napoleon's Great Love* (London: Weidenfeld & Nicholson, 1979).

16 Piotr S. Wandycz, *The Lands of Partitioned Poland* (Seattle: University of Washington Press, 1975).

17 Robert F. Leslie, *Polish Politics and The Revolution of November 1830* (London: Athlone Press, 1956). Angela T. Pienkos, *The Imperfect Autocrat. Grand Duke Constantine Pavlovitch and the Polish Kingdom* (New York: Columbia UP, 1987).

18 Joan Skurnowicz, *Romantic Nationalism and Liberalism. Joachim Lelewel and the Polish National Idea* (New York: Columbia UP, 1981). Andrzej Walicki, *Philosophy and Romantic Nationalism. The Case of Poland* London: Clarendon Press, 1982). On 1863 see Robert F. Leslie, *Reform and Insurrection in Russian Poland, 1856–65* (London: Athlone Press, 1963).

19 Stanislas A Blejwas, *Realism in Polish Politics: Warsaw Positivism and National Survival in the Nineteenth Century* (New Haven, CT: Yale Concilium, 1984).

20 John J. Kulczycki, *School Strikes in Prussian Poland, 1901–1907: The Struggle for Bilingual Education* (New York: Columbia UP, 1981).

21 Cf. Alvin M. Fountain, *Roman Dmowski: Party, Tactics, Ideology, 1895–1907* (Boulder CO: Columbia UP, 1980). Wacław Jędrzejewicz, *Piłsudski. A Life For Poland* (New York: Hippocrene, 1982).

22 Tytus Komarnicki, *Rebirth of the Polish Republic, A Study in the Diplomatic History of Europe, 1914–20* (London: Heineman, 1957). Paul Latawski (ed), *The Reconstruction of Poland, 1914–23* (Basingstoke: Macmillan, 1992).

23 Norman Davies, *White Eagle, Red Star: The Polish-Soviet War , 1919–20* (New York: St. Martin's Press, 1972). Adam Zamoyski, *The Battle for the Marchlands* (New York: Columbia UP, 1981).

24 Marian K. Dziewanowski, *Joseph Piłsudski: A European Federalist, 1918–22* (Stanford: Hoover Institution Press, 1969).

25 George Sakwa, 'The Polish Ultimatum to Lithuania in March 1938', *Slavonic & East European Review*, vol 55, no 2 (April 1977), pp. 204–26.

26 See Raymond L. Buell, *Poland: Key to Europe* (New York: Knopf, 1939). Antony Polonsky, *Politics in Independent Poland, 1921–35* (Oxford: Clarendon Press, 1972). Timothy Wiles (ed), *Poland between the Wars, 1918–45* (Bloomington Ind: Indiana PSC, 1989).

27 Józef Beck, *Final Report* (New York: Robert Speller, 1957).

28 Cf. George Sakwa, 'The Franco-Polish Alliance and The Remilitarisation of the Rhineland', *The Historical Journal*, vol 16, no 1 (March 1973), pp. 125–46.

29 Simon K. Newman, *March 1939: The British Guarantee to Poland* (London: Oxford UP, 1976). Anita Prazmowska, *Britain, Poland and the Eastern Front 1939* (Cambridge: CUP, 1987).

30 Nicholas Bethell, *The War Hitler Won: The Fall of Poland, September 1939* (New York: Holt, 1973). Stephen Zaloga & Victor Madej, *The Polish Campaign 1939* (New York: Hippocrene, 1985).

31   Keith Sword (ed), *The Soviet Takeover of the Polish Eastern Provinces, 1939–1941* (London: Macmillan, 1991).

32   Jan T. Gross, *Polish Society under German Occupation: The General-Gouvernement, 1939–44* (Princeton NJ: Princeton Up, 1979).

33   Richard C. Lukas, *Forgotten Holocaust. The Poles under German Occupation, 1939–44* (Lexington: University Press of Kentucky, 1986).

34   Cf. Antony Polonsky (ed), *My Brother's Keeper? Recent Polish Debates on the Holocaust* (London: Routledge, 1990).

35   Janusz K. Zawodny, *Death in the Forest: The Story of the Katyn Massacre* (Notre Dame Ind: Notre Dame UP, 1962).

36   John Coutouvidis & Jaime Reynolds, *Poland, 1939–47* (Leicester: Leicester UP, 1986). Anita Prazmowska, *Britain and Poland, 1939–1945: The Betrayed Ally* (Cambridge: CUP, 1995).

37   George Kacevitch, *Great Britain, The Soviet Union and the Polish Government-in-Exile, 1939–45* (The Hague: Martinus Nijhof, 1979).

38   Jan Karski, *The Story of a Secret State* (Boston: Houghton Mifflin, 1944). Stanisław Okęcki (ed), *Polish Resistance Movement in Poland and Abroad, 1939–45* (Warsaw: PWN, 1987).

39   Janusz K. Zawodny, *Nothing but Honour. The Story of the Warsaw Uprising 1944* (Stanford Calif: Hoover Institution Press, 1978).

40   Jan Ciechanowski, *The Warsaw Rising of 1944* (Cambridge: CUP, 1974).

41   Antony Polonsky & Bolesław Drukier (eds), *The Beginnings of Communist Rule in Poland* (London: Routledge & Kegan Paul, 1980).

42   Andrzej Paczkowski, *Referendum z 30 czerwca 1946 r.* (Warsaw: ISP PAN, 1993).

43   Krystyna Kersten, *The Establishment of Communist Rule in Poland, 1943–1948* (Berkeley: University of California Press, 1991). Hugh Seton-Watson, *The East European Revolution* (London: Methuen, 1952).

44   Jakub Karpinski, *Countdown. The Polish Upheavals of 1956, 1968, 1970, 1980...* (New York: Karz-Cohl, 1982).

45   George Kolankiewicz & Ray Taras, 'Socialism for Everyman' in A. Brown & J. Gray (eds), *Political Culture and Political Change in Communist States* (London: Macmillan, 1977).

46   Zbigniew Brzezinski, *The Grand Failure* (London: Macdonald, 1990).

47   'Sprawozdanie z prac Komisji KC PZPR powołanej dla wyjaśnienia przyczyn i przebiegu konfliktów społecznych w dziejach Polski Ludowej', *Nowe Drogi*, October 1983.

48   One of the better accounts is Henri Rollet, *La Pologne au XXme Siècle* (Paris: Pedone, 1984). A useful bibliographical guide is Gregory Walker (ed), *Official Publications of the Soviet Union and Eastern Europe, 1945–1980* (London: Mansell, 1982).

49   Richard Hiscocks, *Poland. Bridge for the Abyss* (London: OUP, 1963). Richard F. Staar, *Poland 1944–62: The Sovietization of a Captive People* (Baton Rouge: Louisiana State UP, 1962).

50   Konrad Syrop, *Spring in October. The Story of the Polish Revolution, 1956* (London: Weidenfeld & Nicholson, 1957).

51   Hansjakob Stehle, *The Independent Satellite. Society and Politics in Poland since 1945* (New York: Praeger, 1965).

52   Josef Banas, *The Scapegoats. The Exodus of the Remnants of Polish Jewry* (London: Weidenfeld & Nicholson, 1979).

53   Jerzy Eisler, *Marzec 1968* (Warsaw: PWN, 1991).

54   Zbigniew Pelczynski, 'The Downfall of Gomułka', *Canadian Slavonic Papers*, XV (1973), 1–23. Paweł Domański (ed), *Tajne dokumenty Biura Politycznego. Grudzień 1970* (London: Aneks, 1991).

55   Adam Bromke, *Poland. The Protracted Crisis* (Oakville, Ontario: Mosaic Press, 1983). Keith J. Lepak, *Prelude to Solidarity. Poland and the Politics of the Gierek Era* (New York: Columbia UP, 1988). Paul Lewis, *Political Authority and Party Secretaries in Poland, 1975–86* (Cambridge: CUP, 1982).

56   Michael H. Bernhard, *The Origins of Democratization in Poland* (New York: Columbia UP, 1993). Andrzej Jastrzębski (ed), *Dokumenty Komitetu Obrony Robotników I Komitetu Samoobrony Społecznej 'KOR'* (Warsaw: PWN, 1994). Jan Józef Lipski, *KOR. A History of the Workers' Defense Committee in Poland* (Berkeley: University of California Press, 1985). Peter Raina, *Political Opposition in Poland, 1954–1977* (London: Poet & Painters' Press, 1978): *Independent Social Movements in Poland* (London: Orbis, 1981).

57 For Gierek's later apologias see Janusz Rolicki, *Edward Gierek: Przerwana dekada* (Warsaw: FAKT, 1990) & *Edward Gierek. Replika* (Warsaw: BGW, 1990).

58 Antony Kemp-Welch, *The Birth of Solidarity. The Gdańsk Negotiations 1980* (London: Macmillan, 1983). Cf. *Protokóly porozumień Gdańsk, Szczecin, Jastrzębie...* (Warsaw: KAW, 1981).

59 George Sanford, *Polish Communism in Crisis* (London: Croom Helm, 1983).

60 For the Solidarity period see: Timothy G. Ash, *The Polish Revolution* (London: Jonathan Cape, 1983). Colin Barker, *Festival of the Oppressed. Solidarity, Reform and Revolution In Poland, 1980–81* (London: International Socialism, 1982). Jack Bielasiak & Maurice Simon (Eds), Edge of the Abyss (New York: Praeger, 1984). Michael D. Kennedy, Professionals, Power and Solidarity in Poland (Cambridge: CUP, 1991). Roman Laba, The Roots of Solidarity (Princeton NJ: Princeton UP, 1991). Peter Raina, Towards Socialist Renewal (London: George Allen & Unwin, 1985). Jan de Weydenthal, Bruce Porter & Kevin Devlin, The Polish Drama (Lexington: Lexington Books, 1983). Jean Woodall (ed), Policy and Politics in Contemporary Poland (London: F. Pinter, 1982).

61 Alain Touraine *et al.*, *Solidarity. The Analysis of a Social Movement.* (Cambridge: CUP, 1983). Jadwiga Staniszkis, *Poland's Self-Limiting Revolution* (Princeton NJ: Princeton UP, 1984).

62 George Sanford (ed), *The Solidarity Congress 1981. The Great Debate* (London: Macmillan, 1990).

63 Jacek Kurczewski, *The Resurrection of Rights in Poland* (Clarendon Press: Oxford, 1993).

64 Despite the *post-hoc* explanations of the main figures: Wojciech Jaruzelski, *Stan Wojenny dlaczego...* (Warsaw: BGW, 1992). Stanisław Kania, *Zatrzymać konfrontację* (Warsaw: BGW, 1991). Witold Bereś & Jerzy Skoczylas, *Generał Kiszczak mówi...prawie wszystko* (Warsaw: BGW, 1991).

65 David Ost, *Solidarity and the Politics of Anti-Politics* (Philadelphia: Temple UP, 1990).

66 Leopold Labedz (ed), *Poland under Jaruzelski* (New York: Charles Scribner, 1984). George Sanford, *Military Rule in Poland. The Rebuilding of Communist Power 1981–1983* (London: Croom Helm, 1986).

67 See the political realist justification by Andrzej Walicki, 'The Paradoxes of Jaruzelski's Poland', *Archives Européens de Sociologie*, vol 26, no 1 (1985), pp. 167–92.

68 Lawrence Graham & Maria Ciechocińska (eds), *The Polish Dilemma* (Boulder,CO: Westview, 1987).

69 Andre W. Gerrits, *The Failure of Authoritarian Change: Reform, Opposition and Geo-Politics in Poland in the 1980s* (Aldershot: Dartmouth, 1990). George Kolankiewicz, 'Poland and the Politics of Permissable Pluralism', *East European Politics And Societies*, vol 2, no 1 (1988), pp. 152–83.

70 Cf. Bartołomiej Kamiński, *The Collapse of State Socialism. The Case of Poland* (Princeton NJ: Princeton UP, 1991). George Sanford (ed), *Democratization in Poland, 1988–1990. Polish Voices* (Basingstoke: Macmillan, 1992).

71 Jacek Kuroń & Jacek Żakowski, *PRL dla początkujących* (Wrocław: Wydawnictwo Dolnośląskie, 1996), pp. 281–2.

72 *Spór o PRL* (Kraków: Znak, 1996).

73 Janine Wedel, *Private Poland* (New York: Facts on File, 1986): *The Unplanned Society. Poland after Communism* (New York: Columbia UP, 1992).

74 Mira Marody (ed), *Co nam zostało z tych lat? Społeczeństwo polskie u progu zmiany systemowej* (Warsaw: Aneks, 1991).

Chapter 2

POLITICS IN DEMOCRATIC POLAND

Poland's transformation after 1989 was made up of two dimensions. The first was part of the general regional shift away from communism and towards democracy, the market and Europe. The second was a return to its pre-communist traditions and some aspects of its historical institutional and political dynamics. The latter partly overlapped with the former but it also threw up numerous obstacles to the smooth adaptation of democratic capitalism as well. As we have seen, communism in power soon assumed a national dress in Poland. This meant that many traditional institutions and practices such as the Sejm and the concept of parliamentary sovereignty as well as numerous judicial and administrative bodies not only survived but, also, proved surprisingly easy to re-animate in the democratic era. The same, as it turned out, could not be said for the interwar political parties. Some cultural values were also heavily modified by the modernisation and secularisation aspects of the communist experience.

Four phases can be discerned in Poland's political development since 1989. The first transition stage was marked by the contractual features of the Solidarity takeover of power from the Round Table until Wałęsa's election as president in December 1990, concluding with his conflicts with the Sejm during the Bielecki period. The second stage, that of Solidarity and anti-communist domination ushered in by the 1991 parliamentary elections, saw the very different governments of Olszewski and Suchocka. The third phase, domination by the successor political forces to the tradition of People's Poland, began with the victory of the left and peasant parties in 1993 and was reinforced by Kwaśniewski's election as president in 1995. The political cycle turned around again with the September 1997 parliamentary election. This produced a majority for a government composed of Solidarity and nationalist-Catholic figures claiming their legitimacy from the tradition of the political forces opposed to communism in 1989. Whether they would prove more capable than their predecessors of completing the systemic transformation began in 1989 remained to be seen.

There has been an intense political science debate about whether the defeat of communism would be followed by a direct and immediate process of building a liberal political and market system or whether the future was more open.[1] Authoritarian, early transitional and mixed alternatives are still very much on the agenda in the Balkans and the post-Soviet space.[2] In

Poland, however, what is striking is the speed with which the issue of democratic transition or systemic transformation has been resolved. The question currently being debated is the mainstream one of whether democratic consolidation has already taken place [Taras 1995]. Specialists also wonder about the flexibility of the general democratic capitalist model. Can East European regional variants produce acceptable syntheses to accomodate national cultural and historical traditions or will local values vanish into the maw of global capitalism in the post-communist age? The issue is confused by a dispute, on two quite separate levels, between neo-liberals and social democrats; the general essentials and speed of systemic transformation, especially in the economic sphere, concern systemic change while the final desirable balance between state and society is quite another, and very much normal, aspect of intra-systemic discussion.[3]

The communist authorities abdicated power in a wholly negotiated and contitutional manner in 1989. They lost control of their initial offer of power-sharing because of the unexpected turn of domestic and communist bloc developments. The historical background has already been established while there is good coverage of the social, psychological and the electoral-psephological aspects.[4] Much of the detail on the course of the Round Table has also been elucidated. In addition, the "mechanisms created at the Round Table have survived the transition and have taken on a life of their own', particularly the presidency and the Senate and what one might call the Round Table method of defusing political and social conflicts.[5]

The Round Table only met twice in a full plenary session of all 57 main participants at the beginning of the process on 6 February 1989 and at its completion on 5 April. The main work took place in the three main committees on union pluralism (chairmen: Mazowiecki/Kwaśniewski), political reform (chairmen Geremek/Reykowski) and socio-economic and systemic reform (chairmen Trzeciakowski/Sekuła-Baka jointly), involving 122 negotiators and experts. There were also another 11 working-groups and sub-tables on legal and judicial reform, the media, local government, associations, education, youth policy, housing, agriculture, mining, health care and the environment (involving over 400 discussants). Nevertheless, one should remember that not all the opposition was included in this process. Given the scale of the process in terms of its length and the numbers involved it is hardly surprising that an informal steering mechanism emerged; about a dozen secret meetings between Kiszczak and Wałęsa and their top teams were held at an interior ministry villa in the Warsaw suburb of Magdalenka. Although tales of secret deals, allegedly brokered by Roman Catholic mediators, proliferated these meetings were mainly instrumental in resolving deadlocks and facilitating compromises at the open tables.[6] Splits and disagreements also emerged within the government-coalition side between the PZPR, its minor party ZSL and SD allies and, above all, the increasingly autonomous OPPZ trade union confederation led by Alfred Miodowicz. The same occurred within the so-called Solidarity-opposition between its varied components as well as between its trade union and adviser elements. This allowed for a general bargaining process to develop on the basis of cross-cutting coalitions.

The Round Table resulted in a long and detailed agreement.[7] Only the main political provisions proved crucial as the proposed reform guidelines for specific sectors were largely rendered irrelevant by the subsequent communist abdication. The key political points were that Solidarity, Rural Solidarity and the Independent Students' Union (NZS) were re-legalised without any restrictions; freedom of speech, publication and organisation were conceded as a prelude to the holding of contractual elections to the Sejm and totally-free elections to a newly re-established Senate of 100 in June. The Sejm was to be elected collegially with 60% of the seats being assured to the PZPR (which was to hold just under a majority) and its ZSL and SD allies, another 5% to pro-government Catholic groupings while 35% could be fought over by Solidarity and other opposition movements. The original mathematics of the exercise was designed to give the communists and their allies an overall majority in the Sejm and Senate. It was generally understood, although not written down, that this majority would elect Jaruzelski to the newly established presidency which would have strong executive powers especially in foreign and security matters. Jaruzelski's reformist camp genuinely believed that their historical experiment in guided and controlled democracy would thus gain sufficient social support to enable them to hold their own in the elections and to dominate the subsequent coalition and power-sharing arrangements [Gebethner in Sanford 1992]. Solidarity considered that it might take between two to four years for the mixed system, which had many parallels to 1945–47, to take a decisive turn in their favour. That both were proved so decisively and so quickly wrong merely confirms the unpredictable and cunning workings of Minerva and her owl, a much used metaphor by analysts of this period!

THE CONTRACTUAL TRANSITION

The June 1989 election campaign was an unclear muddle with numerous candidates being presented by the government coalition in contrast to the mainly single civic committee candidates for each available seat endorsed by

Wałęsa in the famous poster-photograph of the time. The results, however, marked an overwhelming psychological sea-change and led to the irreversible political defeat of communism in Poland. The civic committee won 99 out of the 100 Senate seats, all of the 50 provinces right across the country except Piła, joining in what amounted to the universal plebiscitary rejection of communism. On a 62% turnout the civic committee won 160 of the Sejm seats available to it on the first ballot and the remaining one on the second ballot. It not only eliminated all its opposition competitors entirely but its endorsement ensured the election of some of the 19 ZSL and 7 SD deputies who subsequently either voted against, or abstained, in Jaruzelski's election as president. Even more humiliatingly, all bar 2 of the 35 communist notables on the National List, including Kiszczak, Rakowski and Miodowicz, failed to get elected by getting less than the required 50% vote; they were eliminated from the additional run-off. The government-coalition candidates on the second ballot were also elected with humiliatingly low support, often of less than 20%.[8]

All this meant that Jaruzelski was only elected as president on 19 July due to carefully calculated Solidarity abstentions. Kiszczak, although nominated as prime minister found the political tide flowing against him. He failed to form a government as did other last minute suggestions such as Roman Malinowski, the ZSL chairman. After much manoeuvring the ZSL and SD ditched Kiszczak and thus swung the balance of political forces against the PZPR. Wałęsa, in early August, endorsed Adam Michnik's earlier proposal that Solidarity should form a government, set out in his famous article entitled 'Your president—Our prime minister' in the daily *Gazeta Wyborcza* (4 July1989). Tadeusz Mazowiecki (born 1927), who was preferred to Bronisław Geremek (born 1932) and Jacek Kuroń, thus became the first non-communist prime minister of Poland since the fellow-travelling socialist (PPS) Osóbka-Morawski (1909–1997) in 1947. The Sejm endorsed his Grand Coalition, including 4 communists, notably Kiszczak at the interior and General Florian Siwicki at defence, overwhelmingly on 24 August. Foreign affairs went to the Catholic non-party law professor Krzysztof Skubiszewski (born 1926); the Solidarity liberals, notably Leszek Balcerowicz (born 1947), at finance, gained control of the economic and social ministries. They inherited a situation of galloping hyperinflation unleashed by Rakowski's freeing of prices in August.

What is often forgotten nowadays is that this government had to work within Round Table limits. The contractual Sejm survived until 1991, the communist ministers continued until June 1990 and Jaruzelski was only replaced by Wałęsa as president in December 1990. Poland's anti-communist trail-blazing was thus achieved at the cost of initially slow and partial system-ic transformation. In practice many of the external constraints dissolved with the dramatic collapse of the remainder of the East European communist bloc in Autumn 1989. The democratic order was confirmed by the constitutional amendment of December 1989 which abolished the PZPR's leading-role. The Polish Republic, colloquially known as the Third Republic, replaced the Polish People's Republic which was consigned to the dustbin of history. The Rule of Law and constitutional government was established remarkably quickly on the basis of Poland's older civic traditions. The judiciary, procuracy, local government, state bureaucracy and the new civil police (ex-Citizens' Militia ORMO) were verified; the old guard was dismissed, retired early or side-tracked. Communist Party bodies vanished in the now depoliticised Army and factories while the ZOMO and the security police were shrunk with the latter being reformed as the Bureau for State Protection (UOP). The local elections of May 1990 gave the civic committees 41.47% of the seats compared to 40% for (mainly rightwing) non-party candidates and 5.76% for the Peasant Party. Jaruzelski behaved impeccably as the indispensible 'swing-man' in this systemic transformation. He guaranteed its non-victim-isation character domestically, and its residual stability within the dying War-saw Pact with the erstwhile Soviet patron, externally. On the other hand Balcerowicz' big-bang marketisation broke Poland's hyperinflation and achieved the domestic convertability of the *złoty* during 1990. The conse-quences were a dramatic 30% decline in industrial production and an explo-sive rise in unemployment causing massive social discontent.

The PZPR wound itself up in January 1990 handing over the bulk of its supporters to the Social Democracy of the Polish Republic (SdRP) which elected young leaders such as Aleksander Kwaśniewski (born 1954) in a bid to distance itself from the PZPR's sins. Its pro-Solidarity wing, the Polish Social Democratic Union (PUS), led by Tadeusz Fiszbach, the failed reformist throwback from 1981, only survived as a short-lived faction of ersthwhile PZPR deputies in the 1989–91 Sejm. The communist party *aktyw,* at both the institutional and the social levels, had fragmented and decomposed dur-ing 1989. They now vanished completely with their membership mainly withdrawing from political life or joining the successor-communist forces.

The vacuum left by the foregoing was to some extent filled by Solidarity's network of civic committees which were now run by Wałęsa's nominee, Zdz-isław Najder, an ex-Radio Free Europe director. Solidarity's political leader-ship in the national civic committee (KO) and the parliamentary civic committee (OKP), chaired by Bronisław Geremek, continued to share influ-ence with the movement's, Gdańsk based trade union National Executive

Committee (KKW). Wałęsa, who had been marginalised politically since Summer 1989, was re-elected as chairman of the latter body by Solidarity's second congress in Spring 1990. He now opened up a demagogic and populist campaign for the accelerated liquidation of the communist system and its *nomenklatura* from all walks of life. The main demand for early presidential elections raised few difficulties. Jaruzelski agreed to go voluntarily when the communist ministers left the coalition in Summer 1990. So the main conflict, the so-called 'War at the Top', lay within the Solidarity conglomerate. It had maintained its unity for so long by refusing incorporation within the communist system but with the latter's demise an accomplished fact it now split into two competing camps. Wałęsa's supporters, notably Jarosław Kaczyński (born 1949) the editor of *Tygodnik Solidarność* and his twin-brother Lech, set-up the Centre Alliance (*Porozumienie Centrum*) to work for their patron's election as president. Two major regional Solidarity figures, Zbigniew Bujak (born 1954) from Warsaw and Władysław Frasyniuk (born 1954) from Wrocław, formed the Democratic Action 'Civic Movement (ROAD) which was supported by Michnik's *Gazeta Wyborcza*. They backed Mazowiecki for the presidency; what divided the two camps, however, was more a matter of style and personality and the speed of reform and purge of old communists rather than fundamental divergences.

Poland adopted the Gaullist system of the direct election of the president by universal suffrage on 25 November; the top two candidates went forward to a second ballot a fortnight later in the absence of an overall majority. Six candidates, who had collected the required 100,000 signatures for nomination, stood. Poland's political class was well aware of Wałęsa's (born 1943) personal and character defects (laziness, incapacity to understand briefing papers or to keep to them, vainglorious boasting, inconsistency and irresponsible outbursts); such traits, although common people felt that he had his heart in the right place, raised serious doubts as to his suitability for the presidential office with all its serious diplomatic and executive responsibilities.[9] This knowledge had spread widely throughout society as result of his campaigning style; it was no surprise, except to uncritical Western admirers who only saw him in terms of his great historical role as the national symbol of opposition to communism and Nobel Peace Prize winner in 1983, that he only got 39.96% of the first ballot vote.

The real shock, however, was that Mazowiecki with 18.8% was eliminated by Stanisław Tymiński, a completely unknown *emigré* millionaire, who had made his money in Canada and Peru; he received 23.1%. Of the others Włodzimierz Cimoszewicz (born 1950), the personable leader of the SdRP Sejm deputies' club got 9.21 %, Roman Bartoszcze (born 1946), the Polish

Peasant Party (PSL) chairman got 7.15 % and Leszek Moczulski (KPN leader), a mere 2.5%. Wałęsa, supported by Mazowiecki who resigned as prime minister after his humiliating rebuff, defeated Tymiński easily enough with 74.25% of the second ballot vote. The latter's success raised fears that he represented the ex-communist security services and a *poujadist* electoral backlash against the socio-economic costs of the transformation. Analysts were more optimistic in discerning three distinct electorates, at this time, which reflected the complexity and differing experiences of the social transformation: Wałęsa's vote was based on the Roman Catholic peasant and working class areas of Galicia and the big cities; Mazowiecki's drew on the prosperous urban professional and intelligentsia sectors notably in Greater Poland; while Tymiński appealed to anti-Solidarity and declining Poland, especially heavy industry and mining areas threatened by unemployment.[10]

Wałęsa's election, however, marked only the beginning of the end of the first phase in Poland's post-communist development; this was completed by the holding of fully free elections in October 1991 and the promulgation of the 'Little Constitution' in November 1992. The interim was seen through by the government of Jan Krzysztof Bielecki (born 1951), a prominent figure in the Gdańsk based Liberal Democratic Congress (KLD) who became prime minister after a bid by the 1980s dissident lawyer, Jan Olszewski (born 1930) had failed. Bielecki's cabinet retained Balcerowicz in charge of the economy and Skubiszewski at foreign affairs while Admiral Kołodziejczyk, who had replaced the communist Siwicki, stayed on as suitably transitional figure at defence. The greater emphasis on privatisation brought new personalities such as Janusz Lewandowski (born 1951) at ownership transformation and Michał Boni at labour to the fore. Wałęsa's Centre Party supporters Jerzy Eysymontt, Adam Glapiński and Krzysztof Żabiński were rewarded while another budding party, the Christian National Union (ZChN) was represented by its leader Wiesław Chrzanowski (born 1923) at justice.

Bielecki lacked solid political support as the Sejm was still made up of deputies elected by the Round Table contract. The left, although divided, went into formal opposition while the OKP split with Mazowiecki's ROAD supporters forming the Democratic Union (UD). Bielecki also had unclear and erratic relations with Wałęsa's presidential chancellory headed by Jarosław Kaczyński. Balcerowicz's financial austerity and stringency, notably the *popiwek* limiting state-sector wage-increases, and unemployment rising to 1.6 million in the Summer and over 2 million by the end of the year, provoked growing strikes. Marian Krzaklewski (born 1950), a computer programmer from Upper Silesia and Wałęsa's successor as Solidarity chairman, had been elected against his favoured nominees, and took an increasingly independent trade unionist line. Although the government had some foreign policy successes the Sejm refused to give it emergency powers to accelerate marketisation and privatisation. It also overode Wałęsa's presidential vetoes and forced him to sign an electoral law based on an extreme form of proportional representation. Deadlock was reached in August when the Sejm rejected deep expenditure cuts in the state budget. The political atmosphere worsened as a result of notorious scandals such as the Art-B, Grobelny, alcohol and cigarette affairs. Only the KLD and the UD supported Balcerowicz's rigorous financial stabilisation measures. Bitter social conflicts over education, health, police and pensions shortfalls and cuts made it clear that an apathetic and disillusioned electorate could be offered little short-term comfort by the new political parties limbering up for the 1991 election which the contractual Sejm had delayed, to Wałęsa's dismay, till 27 October.[11]

THE NEW FORCES IN POWER (LATE 1991-SEPTEMBER 1993)

Political demobilisation and fragmentation, the key features of the first transitional phase, were at their most marked in the 1991 election. Turnout was only 43.2% but even this included 5.63% spoilt or invalid votes reflecting profound social discontent at the economic costs of transformation and disillusioment with its political aspects. There were attempts to form broader electoral alliances, notably by the SdRP which ran as the Alliance of the Democratic Left (SLD) and the ZChN which formed the Catholic Election Action (WAK), but in the end 90 parties formed 65 electoral lists which presented candidates in more than one constitutency while another 70 electoral committees fought single constituencies. The electoral law to the Senate remained similar to that in 1989 with each province electing 2 Senators except Warsaw and Katowice province which had three; the system now really became 'first past the post' with the abolition of the second ballot. The bitterly fought over, and not wholly coherent, Sejm electoral law laid down that 391 deputies would be elected in 37 electoral districts by proportional representation; the remaining 69 (with easements for national minority parties) would be drawn from a National List from parties who had achieved a 5% hurdle.[12] Altogether 6,980 candidates were nominated for the Sejm and 612 for the Senate:

Sejm election of 27 October 1991 (State Electoral Commission Bulletin, *Rzeczpospolita*, 4 November 1991).

	% of vote	Total seats
Democratic Alliance (UD)	12.31	62
Alliance of Democratic Left (SLD)	11.98	60

Catholic Electoral Alliance (WAK)	8.73	49
PSL 'Programme Alliance'	8.67	48
Confederation for an Independent Poland (KPN)	7.5	46
Centre Alliance (PC)	8.71	44
Liberal Democratic Congress (KLD)	7.48	37
Peasant Alliance	5.46	28
NSZZ Solidarity	5.05	27
Polish Friends of Beer Party	3.27	16
German Minority	1.17	7
Christian Democracy	2.36	5
Christian Democratic Party	1.11	4
Labour Solidarity (SP)	2.05	4
Polish Western Union	0.23	4
Union of Real Politics (UPR)	2.25	3
Party 'X'	0.47	3
Silesian Autonomists	0.35	2

11 other parties or electoral committees won a
seat apiece.

It is technically correct, although misleading, to say that 29 parties were
elected to this Sejm as 9 were local committees standing in a single constituency while only 10 gained double figure representation. The degree of
fragmentation was of more than Fourth French Republic proportions; the
crucial statistic is that the minimum sized majority coalition needed the
support of the 5 largest parties. The UD was more successful in the Senate
gaining 21 seats, followed by Solidarity 12, WAK and Centre Alliance 9
apiece, PSL 8, Peasant Alliance 7, KLD 6, SLD and KPN 4 apiece; 19 other
labels gained the remaining 20 seats. Tymiński's Party X, despite the disqualification of some of its candidates, still managed to show well on purely
populist slogans. Zbigniew Brzezinski's view that fragmentation in 1991
stemmed from an inappropriate electoral law has been refuted. The weakness of the incipient democratic framework and the multiplicity and plastic-
ity of the parties not only made proportional representation inevitable, but
also functionally indispensible.[13]

With the party system in such an incipient and fragmented state, with
political life divided by so many cross-cutting ideological, issue and personality cleavages and with basic questions affecting executive-parliamentary relations being left unresolved until the 'Little Constitution' it is hardly surprising
that coalition-building after the election proved a long drawn-out and complicated affair. The view that 'the major fear generated by the Polish election

result was one of prolonged government instability, possibly leading to authoritarian solutions'may now seem fanciful, but it had some justification at the time.[14]

Wałęsa's first preference for prime minister was Bronisław Geremek (UD). After a false start Jan Olszewski (PC) finally brought a debilitating two months of political paralysis and manoeuvring to some sort of close by forming a government on 21 December but its prospects were weak from the outset. Olszewski only had the full support of the ZChN, the Peasant Alliance and the Centre Alliance with more tenuous backing from the KPN and the KLD. He also had bad personal relations with Wałęsa and never succeeded in achieving an acceptable constitutional basis for sharing executive power with him. Olszewski's inflationary attempt to prime the economy and combat unemployment by increasing state subsidies to enterprises led his first finance minister to resign while the Sejm rejected his economic programmme on 5 March 1992.

Olszewski thus became desperate to broaden his coalition and to 'settle acounts' with the communist period through accelerated decommunisation in the personnel field. But he proved an emotional and maladroit politician. He came into basic conflict with three crucial forces—the military, the parliamentary and administrative elite and the presidency—who brought about his downfall. He was also badly served by his ministerial supporters notably Jan Parys, the first civilian minister of defence, and Antoni Macierewicz (born 1948), the minister of the interior, a fiery colleague from the national independence struggle against communist power. Parys provoked a conflict with Wałęsa over the issue of control of the Army. Parys pensioned off his predecessor, Admiral Kołodziejczyk, in January and rejected proposals for the reorganisation of the National Security Council. He threatened the officer corps with a complete purge of all communist influences. In April he went too far by accusing Mieczysław Wachowski, Wałęsa's presidential chief of staff, close confidant and ex-chauffeur—a personality who admittedly was widely regarded as a dangerous and primitive behind the scenes fixer—of having attempted to organise an army plot to bring down the legitimate government. The resultant uproar forced Olszewski to suspend Parys who was eventually dismissed by the Sejm.

The final straw came over the so-called *lustration* affair, the classical term for ceremonial purification. Macierewicz moved to reveal the secret ministry of the interior (MSW) files showing which individuals in public life had collaborated with the communist security services. He sent out sealed envelopes, containing 64 names, to key political figures. As much of the MSW material had already been destroyed, and the remainder was unreliable, a storm developed especially as many ex-dissidents were named. Rumours spread that Wałęsa himself had had contacts with the security agencies and figured under the pseudonym of *Bolek*. On Wałęsa's initiative, the Sejm defeated the government on a vote of no confidence in early June. Wałęsa nominated the Peasant Party (PSL) leader, Waldemar Pawlak (born 1959), as Olszewski's replacement but his time had not yet come. A month of fruitless negotiations revealed the post-Solidarity camp's distrust of his protectionist small peasant electorate which had succeeded the ZSL. Pawlak was unwilling to accept the neo-liberal policies of the UD, KLD and the managerial section of the Beer-Lovers' Party, known as the 'Big Beer'. As the nationalist and Catholic forces had disgraced themselves the pendulum swung back in favour of the UD. Under pressure of the usual unpolished threats from Wałęsa the parliament produced an inspired nomination who, most unexpectedly, stabilised the democratisation process by steering Poland out of political paralysis and *Sejmocracy* and into the golden uplands of economic up-turn.

Hanna Suchocka (born 1946), a Poznań University law lecturer, had as an SD Sejm deputy in the early 1980s abstained in the symbolic 1981 vote on martial law. Emerging through ROAD and Geremek's patronage she reflected the complex nuances of Polish politics; the first female prime minister in Poland's history demonstrated a steady temperament and a balanced character. She managed to form and maintain fairly solid seven party support made up of the hard-core UD, KLD and 'Big Beer' so-called Little Coalition plus the ZChN and three peasant and christian democratic fractions. By remaining neutral over the highly contentious abortion dispute she also had general Solidarity and Centre Party support. The PC decamped from her coalition and became increasingly fractious because of the Kaczyński brothers' venomous quarrel with Wałęsa. Her cabinet was also based on major experienced figures notably Kuroń (labour), Skubiszewski (foreign affairs), Bielecki (Europe), Osiatyński (finance), Janusz Onyszkiewicz (defence) and Gabriel Janowski (agriculture) who represented the Solidarity peasant party strand (PL). Unlike her predecessor Suchocka also established a good working relationship with Wałęsa. This allowed the smoothing over of the final stages of the passing of the 'Little Constitution' into law by November.

The personable Suchocka built up her standing and restored Poland's reputation abroad through a series of well-publicised foreign visits. But economic discontent at home remained rife with numerous strikes during the second half of 1992 especially by copper and coal miners and in the Tychy car factory. The countryside was also in turmoil through the protests of Andrzej Lepper's Self-Defence movement (*Samoobrona*) which organised repossessed and indebted peasants into direct action. The government responded by loosening the *popiwek* and Kuroń established a social contract through a Trilateral Pact. The situation was stabilised by some economic improvement from late 1992 onwards, but at the cost of the fundamental alienation of Solidarity and the other trade union confederations. Walking the tightrope between social discontent and necessary economic restructuring proved an impossible task. Privatisation minister Lewandowski was almost defeated by the Sejm in September, coalition members defended their political patches while the PC and ZChN reverted to populist and demagogic demands for an early presidential election. Solidarity was largely to blame for allowing Suchocka to be defeated by a single vote on the no-confidence issue of 28 May 1993 although she continued *pro tem* until after the election of 19 October.

Solidarity and the anti-communist camp thus somewhat accidently lost power, just as the transformation was beginning to produce benefits as well as costs and just as the tiller was beginning to respond to the direction of its more balanced leaders. But the relapse into bad Polish habits of *Sejmocracy*, cynical political manoeuvring and allegations of corruption, strengthened popular cynicism and alienation. The highly personal quarrel between Wałęsa and the centre-right also went beyond the normal and continuing political dispute over executive-parliamentary relations. It is, therefore, neither surprising nor wholly unjust that the election mood of throwing the rascals out should have swung power back to the centre-left in its successor-communist variant.

SYSTEMIC TRANSFORMATION CONTINUES UNDER THE LEFT-PEASANT GOVERNMENTS (SEPTEMBER 1993–NOVEMBER1995)

The extent of the September swing away from what one might loosely call the 1989 anti-communist camp was, however, caused by highly specific, as well as general, causes. The primary factor was a new electoral law which was regarded as a corrective to the extremes of multipartyism produced by the proportional representation of 1991.[15] The 391 regional seats at issue were now fought over in 52 smaller constituencies instead of 37 but the party lists were distributed by the d'Hondt not Hare-Niemeyer formula. Crucially a minimum 5% threshold had to be achieved by single political parties in order to gain Sejm representation while alliances had to gain a minimum 8%. The qualifying threshold for the National List of 69 seats was increased from 5% to 7%. The effect of this law was to restrict representation in the Sejm to six parties, to eliminate the divided and quarrelling centre-right almost entirely and to exaggerate centre-left representation dramatically. But the party system had already crystallised to the extent that only 12 parties contested every constituency, another 3 fought most of them while altogether 35 electoral committees nominated 8,787 Sejm candidates. Another 684 candidates, slightly more than in 1991, stood for the Senate. Turnout was 52.08% with 4.3% invalid votes in the Sejm election.

Sejm election of 19 September 1993 (Rzeczpospolita, 27 September 1993).

	% vote	Total seats
Alliance of the Democratic Left (SLD)	20.41	171
Polish Peasant Party (PSL)	15.40	132
Democratic Union (UD)	10.59	74
Labour Union (UP)	7.28	41
Confederation for an Independent Poland (KPN)	5.77	22
Non-Party Bloc supporting the Reform (BBWR)	5.41	16

The German Minority also gained 4 seats on a mere 0.41% of the vote, as it did not have to meet any threshold, but it gained the largest vote in Opole province. This contrasted with the failure of the social catholic and economically protectionist Fatherland (*Ojczyzna*) alliance to gain any representation with 6.4% of the vote. Other non-qualifiers were Solidarity 4.9%, PC 4.4%, KLD 4.0% and others 14.8%. This meant that 34.53% of the vote was completely unrepresented while the SLD and PSL with 35.81% of the vote held 303 (65.9%) of the 460 seats. The KPN survived although it lost about half its seats. The UP led by the economist Ryszard Bugaj and Bujak developed out of Labour Solidarity although it opposed economic liberalism and appealed as a 'new' party. Wałęsa's belated attempt to emulate the 1930's Piłsudski-ite formation with his Non-Party Bloc for Supporting the Reform, the BBWR of the same initials, qualified, but fell far short of expectations. Despite an impressive performance by its official leader, ex-finance minister Andrzej Olechowski, it suffered from Wałęsa's populist promises and direct involvement, especially his unconstitutional threat to become prime minister.

The genuine swing to the left took place even more clearly in the Senate election which resulted in 37 seats for the SLD and 36 for the PSL followed by Solidarity 10, UD 4, UP 2, BBWR 2 and 9 other groupings one apiece. Regionally the SLD came first in 29 provinces mainly in the north and west while the PSL ran out top in 20 provinces in the south and east. Suchocka's popularity pushed the UD to the front in Poznań and local factors gave them Kraków as well. The significance of 1993 was not that it marked a communist restoration or threatened democracy, despite much frothy rhetoric to that effect. It was a rejection of Solidarity's economic liberalism and shock-therapy as well as the National Catholic camp's incompetence, disunity and populism. The systemic transformation towards democratic capitalism and

Europe was not endangered although its time-scale was extended and the payment of its costs stretched out.

Given the election results it was inevitable that the new government would be an SLD-PSL coalition. The former acted moderately by allowing Pawlak to become prime minister of the government endorsed on 9 November. In exchange one of its chieftains, Józef Oleksy, become Sejm-Marshal. Wałęsa, having more than succeeded in smashing the right, now had a much weaker position despite nominating Olechowski as foreign minister, Andrzej Milczanowski to the interior and Kołodziejczyk to defence. The UD went into opposition with the KPN while the UP remained semi-independent with one of its members taking over industry.

Kwaśniewski did not join the cabinet but remained dominant behind the scenes in control of the SdRP deputies' club and in charge of the Sejm Commission rewriting the constitution. His movement gained two deputy-prime ministerial posts, Marek Borowski (born 1946) in finance and Cimoszewicz in justice, while labour and social policy went to the leader of the PZPR old guard, Leszek Miller (born 1946) and privatisation, after much dispute with the PSL, to Wiesław Kaczmarek. The PSL held 9 cabinet posts most notably deputy-prime minister Aleksander Łuczak in charge of the state administration and also education minister and Michał Strąk who headed the office of the council of ministers (URM). In policy terms the paradox was that the urban-based successor communists continued market-reform and privatisation in tandem with PSL protection of agriculture. They rode out renewed industrial unrest, this time fomented by Solidarity, which despite causing repeated political crises during 1993–95, eventually exhausted itself with the growing economic up-turn. The SLD also managed to keep its 61 OPZZ Sejm deputies in line depite the more dynamic leadership provided by Ewa Spychalska (born 1949), Miodowicz's successor since late 1991. It ended the cohabitation with its old historical enemy Wałęsa by electing its leader Kwaśniewski to the presidency in November 1995 which assured left domination. One should remember though that the peasant-left regime of 1993–97 went through three sub-phrases denoted by the governments of Pawlak, Oleksy and Cimoszewicz.

.The new political patterns were confirmed by the local elections of June 1994 which, on a normal turnout of 33.8%, returned many independents. The SLD consolidated its hold on many northern and western cities, including Warsaw, and the PSL strengthened its presence in rural areas while right wing parties showed well in eastern Poland.

A wave of strikes, coalition in-fighting and the Silesian Bank scandal led to Borowski's replacement by the non-party Grzegorz Kołodko (born 1949) as deputy-prime minister for the economy and minister of finance in May. Kołodko developed Balcerowicz's achievements in building the market economy. While maintaining rigorous monetary policy he moved on from what he termed the latter's 'creative destruction' in privatisation. He wagered in his *Strategy for Poland* programme that his looser wages policy would be covered by 1994 economic growth which turned out to be about 5% although inflation remained high at 29% and food prices increased even more. Kołodko's nomination over that of the SdRP's Dariusz Rosati (vetoed by Wałęsa) and conflicts over tobacco and bank privatisation and local government reform provoked growing resentment within the SLD. So did Strąk's determined use of URM to place PSL nominees in the state administration and PSL 'colonisation' of economic ministries.

THE 1995 PRESIDENTIAL ELECTION

The political scene was already being dominated by manoeuvring between, and within, parties for the presidential election even though it was still a year ahead. A significant step in this direction had already been taken on the opposition side from late 1993 onwards in the amalgamation of the UD with the KLD in a new Freedom Union (UW) which was formally effected in April 1994. This was led by Mazowiecki until his two-to-one defeat by Balcerowicz at its second congress in April 1995. Pawlak and Wałęsa generally supported each other as over the controversial (and defeated) nomination of an ex-PRL spymaster, Marian Zacharski, to head the UOP in August 1994. This led to in-fighting within the presidential staff in the *Belweder* strengthening Wachowski's position and causing the resignation of Wałęsa's press-spokesman, Andrzej Drzycimski. By late 1994 polls showed that over half the population were dissatisfied with Pawlak; his performance as prime minister and coalition manager was criticised by the political elite. Wałęsa's presidential vote at that time was estimated at only 9% compared to 17% for Kuroń, 14% for Olechowski, 8% for Oleksy. 5% for Suchocka, 3% for Krzaklewski and 2% for Adam Strzembosz (born 1930), the very conservative Solidarity president of the supreme court and, as such, of the state tribunal.

The above factors led Kwaśniewski to criticise the PSL in February 1995 as a wholly protectionist agricultural and office-seeking lobby. On the other hand the majority of the electorate opposed the psychological war against the Sejm implied in Wałęsa's threat of early dissolution. His patronage of the military faction led by the Chief of Staff, General Tadeusz Wilecki, leading to Kołodziejczyk's dismissal from defence, was also part of the wheeler-dealing and budgetary conflict which caused Pawlak's replacement as prime minister by the SdRP's Józef Oleksy (born 1946) in March 1995. The latter's post of Sejm-Marshal went to the balanced and dignified PSL chairman, Józef Zych (born 1938). The coalition continued, however, as the UD and UP, were not willing to negotiate ahead of the presidential election. Oleksy's reconstruct-ed cabinet saw his rival's Cimoszewicz's departure, Kołodko's entrench-ment and the new presidential nominations of the historian Władysław Bartoszewski (born 1922) in foreign affairs and Wojciech Okoński in defence. Miller went to labour, Borowski to URM and Jerzy Jaskiernia to jus-tice on the SLD side. Roman Jagieliński's (born 1947) nomination to agricul-ture was a significant PSL change.

The second presidential election in democratic Poland took place under more normal and settled conditions than its 1990 predecessor. As in America, there was almost a year of preparatory manoeuvring by key politicians to gain their party's nomination even before the campaign proper began in Summer 1995. Seventeen candidates met the registration requirements of 100,000 signatures, although the extremist National Democrat (PWN) right-winger, Bolesław Tejkowski failed to do so, and another two withdrew before the vote. Ten of the officially registered candidates can be character-ised as individual publicity seekers or smaller party figures, like Moczulski, Lech Kaczyński and Janusz Korwin-Mikke (chairman of the ultra free market Union of Real Politics, UPR).

Of the five serious contenders, Kwaśniewski had long been regarded as the main candidate of the left and maintained public opinion poll figures of about 25% support. Endorsed overwhelmingly as the SLD candidate at a nominating convention in late May he hardly put a foot wrong, in a very effective American style electoral campaign. The UW candidate was Kuroń who barely defeated Onyszkiewicz with Suchocka third at its lively second congress in April. Wałęsa's poll ratings and political standing started off from a very low base, of about 77% dissatisfaction with the presidency in a Pentor poll in September; but he took advantage of the divisions of the right and centre which produced multiple nominations by less established candid-ates. This eventually enabled him to break-through, very much *faute de mieux,* as the candidate most likely to defeat Kwaśniewski. But it was a close run-thing. Tadeusz Zieliński (born 1926), the much respected Ombudsman, supported by the UP, and Hanna Gronkiewicz-Waltz (born 1952), the pres-ident of the Polish National Bank, backed by the ZChN, showed very strongly in the early stages of the campaign, as indeed did Kuroń, before falling back. Pawlak enjoyed lukewarm PSL support gaining nomination by only a single vote against Adam Struzik, the Senate-Marshal. Wałęsa fought back strongly from August onwards with his usual demagogic decommunisation slogans and populist campaigning style. He also dismissed Wachowski from his presidential office, cynically and cunningly making him a scapegoat for his own sins. The new minister of state in the presidential office, the highly respected Warsaw University professor, Andrzej Zakrzewski, hastened to reorganise the presidential chancellory and to restore its image.

Kwaśniewski confirmed his position as front-runner by getting 48.8% of the vote to Wałęsa's 12.7% and Kuroń's 9.5% in the now traditional mock primary election held in Września on 15 October. The actual first ballot result on 5 November 1995 on a 65% turnout saw Kwaśniewski nosing ahead of Wałęsa by 35.11% to 33.11%. Kuroń got 9.22%, Olszewski, 6.86%, Pawlak 4.31% and Gronkiewicz-Waltz (2.76%).[16] The UP, PC and PSL remained neutral but the UW rallied to Wałęsa, who enjoyed open Roman Catholic church support because of his anti-abortion stance, in the run-off on 19 November. Despite this Kwaśniewski won by 51.72% of the vote to 48.28% on a higher 68.23% turnout.

Wałęsa, typically, did not go gracefully. He challenged Kwaśniewski's election by claiming that his opponent had transferred funds to his wife, Jolanta, and based his claim to professionalism on the basis of a university degree which he did not have. After the supreme court had rejected the latter objection on 11 December he got his presidentially nominated interior minister, Andrzej Milczanowski (born 1939), to claim, from the Sejm tribune on 21 December, that prime minister Oleksy had maintained contacts with Soviet Intelligence throughout the 1990s; the implication was that he was a traitor and a spy. The affair was to rumble on and to dominate, as well as destabilise, Polish politics for much of 1996. Kwaśniewski won the 1995 election because Poles increasingly viewed politics in normal, less ideological, terms of practical self-interest and political performance; they considered Kwaśniewski superior to Wałęsa in personal style and efficacy as well as in social welfare policy. The rhetoric of the time about the communists returning to power or 1995 being a defeat for the Solidarity camp was misleading. The 1989 camps had long fragmented and been replaced by movements competing more along typically normal left-right, Catholic-secular, urban-rural, class interest and other cleavage lines. Wałęsa did not even have the good manners, and certainly set a bad precedent for Polish political *mores* by not attending his successor's swearing-in. His belated attempt to maintain ideological-systemic divisions and his personal indispensability by polarising political life with the Oleksy affair can now be seen as the desperate last throw of a bad loser at odds with post-communist politics.[17]

THE CAMP OF PEOPLE'S POLAND DOMINATES
(DECEMBER 1995–SEPTEMBER 1997)

Kwaśniewski resigned from the SdRP on election and nominated Danuta Waniek, his campaign manager, as head of the presidential chancellory. Cimoszewicz replaced him in the very important post of chairman of the parliamentary Constitutional Commission and Jerzy Szmajdziński (born 1952) became chairman of the SLD Sejm deputies' club. Oleksy ran his cabinet very effectively during the campaign period and prevented the Miller-Kołodko conflict from getting out of hand. But he was put on the defensive by the spying charges and had to go along with the new presidential nominations of the capable and personable economist Dariusz Rosati to the foreign ministry, Zbigniew Siemiątowski to the interior and Stanisław Dobrzański (PSL) to defence. Miller gained a strategic position for political in-fighting by becoming URM head. The PSL's public opinion rankings weakened while the SLD more than held its own. Rumours of an early parliamentary dissolution or the splitting up of the coalition, therefore, had no basis in political realities. UW-PSL conversations got nowhere in January, the SLD closed ranks while Wałęsa's hopes of uniting the right-centre opposition proved fruitless after the election. Olechowski formed the Movement of One Hundred (RS) for the serious and modern members of the centre-right and Olszewski the Movement for Rebuilding Poland (ROP) for traditionalist ranters. But politics for many months were completely overshadowed by the long-drawn out ramifications of the Oleksy affair.

Milczanowski had built up a strong and judicious reputation so his Sejm statement was taken very seriously. The MSW material which he sent on to the supreme military procurator alleged that Oleksy had consciously collaborated with Soviet security agencies from about 1982 onwards, especially as PZPR First Secretary in Biała Podlaska province in the late 1980s. Given the pseudonym *Olin* he had maintained close and continuing contacts with two Soviet, and later, Russian agents in Warsaw. As Sejm-Marshal, he had been warned off by the UOP against seeing one of them, later identified as Vladimir Alganov, the Secretary of the Russian Embassy. His failure to break off social contacts was considered as unwise from the outset but specific charges of handing over state information remained to be investigated. Oleksy denied all allegations of wrong-doing but left himself open to further attack by claiming that the UOP material had been *largely* fabricated.

The Sejm set up a Special Commission headed by UP chairman Bugaj, to investigate the matter. Under growing PSL pressure and losing public confidence Oleksy had to resign as prime minister. His party recognising that its own standing was linked to his political survival refused to abandon him before charges were proved. The Special Sejm Commission cleared the way for him to become SdRP chairman by stating in its preliminary report that while the security agencies had acted correctly no substantive evidence of wrong-doing had, as yet, emerged. As early as March he seemed to be home and dry. Rumours spread that the supreme military procuracy would soon complete the investigation. Whether this was linked with the resignation of UOP head General Gromosław Czempiński and the postponement of demands for the publication of a White Book of documents on the affair was unclear. In the event the investigation was suspended in late April by Sławomir Gorzkie-wicz, the Warsaw military district procurator. He was immediately assailed for leaving the substantive issue of Oleksy's guilt in the Scottish state of 'non-proven' and for revealing the role of a Russian officer, Grigory Jakimiszyn, who had been recruited by Polish Intelligence. A CBOS poll showed that 34% thought that Oleksy was innocent as against 29% who were convinced of his guilt; only 40% felt that the matter had been clarified satisfactorily.

The Sejm Commission did not report until Autumn by which time the left had reversed the issue of responsibility by attacking Milczanowski for reveal-ing state secrets. Attempts were made to arraign him before the state tribu-nal. The White Book, when published in October, included no definite proof either way.[18] The volume left the impression that Oleksy was guilty of polit-ical irresponsibility as he had maintained old habits and social and alcoholic contacts with known Russian agents after the fall of communism in both Poland and the USSR,. Finally, the Sejm Commission after ten months work in November produced a majority report which castigated the UOP for breaking the law and a minority report which stated that it had, merely, not followed the correct procedural rules.

The new prime minister, Włodzimierz Cimoszewicz belonged to Kwaś-niewski's pragmatic and social liberal wing. As vice-Marshal he had built a Sejm reputation for independence and cooperation across party lines. He was now expected to clean up the political scene, to consolidate the govern-ing coalition, to initiate a new economic course and to strengthen the SdRP's social democratic character. Half of OBOP respondents welcomed his nom-ination against under a fifth who opposed it. The electorate showed much less enthusiasm in the referendum on privatisation which only achieved a 32.4% turnout and not the required 50%, therefore, having no binding effect upon the government. The most important of the five changes in his cabinet reshuffle was the replacement of Jerzy Jaskiernia at justice, who had caught much of the flak from the Oleksy affair, by Leszek Kubicki. Jerzy Wiatr (born 1931), the well-known reform-communist intellectual, became minister of national education.

The Kwaśniewski-Cimoszewicz tandem quickly gained majority public opinion support and benefitted from such events as the enthusiastic reception given to the state visit of Queen Elisabeth II of Great Britain to Poland in early April. Kwaśniewski's wife, Jolanta, an elegant brunette and Gdańsk University law graduate, also emerged as a genuinely popular First Lady. She modelled herself on Danielle Mitterrand but was more often compared to Hillary Clinton, especially after the latter's private visit to Poland in July 1996.[19] But the SLD lost popularity giving rise to rumours of early parliamentary elections. Kołodko's revised economic programme was unveiled to offset this. His 'Package 2000' forecast dynamic economic growth, a rise in exports and a significant decline in inflation and unemployment; the much contested income tax rates remained at the 1995 figures of 20, 31 and 43%

The government was also rent internally over two proposed, institutional reforms, central and local, the first of which had been initiated by Suchocka. The amalgamation of URM with the interior ministry was proposed leaving a prime minister's chancellory but UOP was now to be subordinated directly to the prime minister. This super-ministry was envisaged as satisfying Miller's ambitions although it was December before he was actually nominated. This also formed part of a wider reform of the central, mainly industrial, ministries. The main changes were that the central planning office (CUP) was replaced by a centre for strategic studies while ministries for the economy and for the state treasury took the place of industry and commerce, ownership transformation and economic collaboration abroad. A new committee for European integration was to prepare more comprehensively for EU entry. The second involved the draft reform of local government where SLD pressure for the restoration of the old pre-1973 counties (*powiaty*) met with unrelenting and paralysing PSL opposition.

Danuta Waniek also brought the coalition's disquiet at General Wilecki's over-close relations with Wałęsa into the open. Their attempt to reorganise the General Staff and to increase civilian control and prevent duplication as laid down by the late 1995 Law on the ministry of defence (MON) was complicated by Onyszkiewicz's (UW) refusal to enter the National Security Council. It took till December before Dobrzański cut Wilecki down to size by laying down that the Chief of Staff's powers would be defined by the minister of defence. It was March 1997 before Kwaśniewski dismissed him from his post and replaced him with General Henryk Szumski, an adviser in his National Security Bureau. A predictable domestic political storm arose as Szumski had gained promotion after commanding the tank division which broke down the gates of the Warski shipyard in Szczecin during martial law pacification by the ZOMO on 14–15 December 1981. His appointment was paradoxically viewed as facilitating NATO entry. His new team accepted the slimming down of the Polish Army from 230,000 to 180,000 by 2004 and heeded American arguments on the need for 100 new fighters to replace ageing MiG's; this led to an agreement in Spring 1997 on the assembly of the Lockheed F-16 fighter at the PZL plant in Mielec.

The proposed closure of Solidarity's holy shrine, the Gdańsk shipyard, which had undergone numerous ownership and restructuring proposals, caused the normal sit-in strike in May 1996. Its 'final' liquidation in March 1997, when the official receiver started dismissing the remaining 3,700 workers, was postponed. A violent Solidarity demonstration in Warsaw on 19 March induced the government to reprieve the badly mismanaged economic white elephant, yet again. The yard received a contract to build 5 ships for the state-owned PZM shipping company in exchange for wider agreement to the restructuring of a new shipbuilding conglomerate headed by Szczecin.

Summer 1996 also saw a complicated exchange between the Roman Catholic church and Kwaśniewski over the ratification of the Concordat signed by Suchocka in Spring 1993, which had been postponed for so long. Primate Józef Glemp (born 1929) and his advisers seem to have overplayed their financial and property restitution demands. The SdRP did not follow Kwaśniewski's wishes as they wanted a bilateral declaration to define the Concordat; yet another favourable moment passed when the Sejm voted by a majority of 29 in mid-July 1996 to postpone ratification until after the passing of the new constitution. The leftist majority in the Sejm provoked the church further by voting, against the Senate's objection, to legalise abortion on social grounds. This law was, however, declared unconstitutional by the constitutional tribunal in a controversial judgment in May 1997. Negotiations were renewed especially when Kwaśniewski met the Pope in the Vatican in early April 1997. After that, Kwaśniewski and the Sejm refused demands for a referendum on abortion on the grounds that it would be a divisive distraction at election time.

The government's slowing down of economic reform and privatisation, already very marked in the protection of coal and steel, now showed itself in the petrol sector. A shortage occurred during Summer 1996 while petrol prices were not freed until the following Spring. The public was disillusioned by the continual horse-trading between the SLD and the PSL over influence and benefits. The latter's corruption in the offices which they controlled caused the resignation of foreign trade minister Jacek Buchacz in September. At that time a CBOS poll showed that 54% thought that the goverment was reforming Poland too slowly, 20% at the right speed and only 6% saw too much speed. On the other hand a number of historically sensitive controversies were gently laid to rest in the Autumn. Colonel Ryszard Kukliński's 1984 death-sentence *in absentia* for treason for spying for the USA since 1970 and for handing over the plans for martial law in Autumn 1981 was laid aside. The Sejm also decided to freeze proceedings on the constitutional responsibility for the State of War against 15 surviving members of WRON and the Council of State. The two MO policemen who had beaten up and killed the student, Grzegorz Przemyk, in a 1980s *cas célèbre* were also finally sentenced, although somewhat symbolically, in April 1997.

The first year of Kwaśniewski's presidency was generally considered successful because of his conciliatory and personable style, the high rate of economic growth and the successes which Poland achieved internationally. He was the runner-up to Wiesława Szymborska, the poetess who had just won the Nobel Prize for Literature, in the annual plebiscite for the Pole of the Year in 1996. CBOS polls showed that on taking office 53% had approved of him while after a year this figure had increased to 58% but the disapproval level had increased from 12% to 22%. Similar figures after a year in office had been 36% for and 42% against for Jaruzelski and 38% for and 46% against for Wałęsa. The slowing down of structural reform and the continual manoeuvring between the coalition partners were the most criticised debits.

Something like an organised opposition emerged with Solidarity 'Electoral Action' (AWS) which by Spring 1997 grouped Solidarity, the KPN, the ZChN, the PL plus numerous Catholic and rightwing parties under Krzaklewski's chairmanship. Its poll ratings nudged up towards a quarter of the electorate and remained roughly equal to the SLD's rankings. The government coalition partners thus had to face up to the possibility of a serious electoral challenge in the 1997 parliamentary elections. The UW congress confirmed its independent centrist stance hostile to the SLD and PSL but also its unwillingness to go beyond a non-aggression pact with the AWS. There was even a degree of coalescence in the notoriously fissiparous conservative-nationalist camp. Miller's replacement as minister of labour by the non-party and highly respected ex-Ombudsman, Tadeusz Zieliński (whose own post was filled by another non-related Zieliński, Adam) was interpreted as an attempt to appeal to the middle ground.

The big surprise in February 1997 was Kołodko's resignation and his replacement by one of Kwaśniewski's advisers, Marek Belka. This was due to growing conflicts with Miller and Cimoszewicz and the loss of Kwaśniewski's support. The non-party, and outspoken Kołodko was, perhaps, justified in claiming credit for the economic up-turn. During his tenure GDP had increased by about 20%, at the rate of 6% per annum, average income had increased by 70%, inflation had fallen from 29% to 19% and the ratio of public debt to GDP had fallen from 86% in 1993 to 49% in 1996. The SLD hierarchy now decided to make Cimoszewicz their 'electoral locomotive' in the parliamentary election campaign thus hoping to gain direct party credit from the growing economic prosperity. Kołodko made costly mistakes like the gift allowance in the income tax provisions and left Poland with large and growing budget and trade deficits; but his achievements were on a par with those of Balcerowicz.

Belka took office on condition that he be allowed to renew the privatisation drive and to push through a pensions reform involving a shift from the pay-as-you go to a fund based system. Poland had an ageing population and 9.2 million pensioners in 1996. Their generously indexed pensions needed topping-up to the extent that such payments made up of over 15% of the state budget. The proposed reform, overseen by a special plenipotentiary, the Kraków economics professor, Jerzy Hausner, set up a mixture of compulsory and voluntary investment funds and raised money through privatisation bonds. Belka also promised that a 5% growth rate and a decline in inflation from 19% to 13% would balance the budget and cover a worrying increase in the trade deficit to $6 billion (4% of GDP). Privatisation went ahead with a very successful sale of the Commercial Bank and of residual state holdings in other banks as well as the quoting of 15 national investment funds on the Warsaw stock exchange in May.

One of Kołodko's last acts, the re-imposition of 20% customs charges on imported cereal fodder had, however, ignited a bitter personal power-struggle within the PSL. It drew attention to the backward state of Polish agriculture which employed 26.9% of the workforce but only produced 6% of GNP. Roman Jagieliński, led the PSL's reformist wing favouring the capitalist transformation of the countryside. He gained the agriculture ministry as a result of Pawlak's poor showing in the presidential election. Jagieliński had the support of the 160,000 farm units of over 10 hectares in size, mainly in northern and western Poland. Pawlak's populist and preservationist wing represented the interests of the decaying 1.8 million family farms below 6.7 hectares mainly in Catholic south and eastern Poland. About half of these were held to be unviable and due to be liquidated before EU entry. At the PSL congress in February 1997 Pawlak's majority withdrew Jagieliński's party recommendation and forced him to resign. He was replaced, after much delay, by Pawlak's close supporter, Jarosław Kalinowski (born 1962) who had to promise to continue the existing agricultural policy. All this allowed Pawlak to gain control of candidate nomination within the PSL; but it also contributed to the party's overall electoral weakening.

Olszewski's ROP collected the required 500,000 signatures and demanded a parallel referendum on their so-called 'civic' version of the constitution. They were denied, with little controversy outside their own circles, as this went against the previously agreed parliamentary procedure. The final stages of work on the new constitution were dominated by religious issues in early 1997 namely the inclusion of the right to life for the foetus and the reference to God Almighty in the preamble. The National Assembly achieved the compromises necessary for majority support (450 to 41 with 6 abstentions on the final version including presidential amendments) in early April despite the agitation of Father Tadeusz Rydzyk's Radio Maryja which gained much publicity for the Enthronement of Christ the King in the constitution. Another divide thus opened up on the opposition side between the UW, the UP and the PSL who finally agreed the constitutional draft with the SLD and the AWS and national-Catholic right who remained obdurately convinced that 'God had been thrown out of the constitution' as they quaintly put it. The 288th Episcopal Conference of the Roman Catholic church left the referendum vote open to individual conscience. But it also stated that the church harboured serious moral reservations about certain provisions. This was reiterated publicly by many of its priests. Kwaśniewski called on all Poles to support the constitution in the referendum but only 52.71% heeded his call on a 42.86% turnout on 25 May. Support reflected the divide between the modernising north and west and the stagnant south and east. The constitution gained less than 40% support in 7 and only 40–50% in another 8 of the latter provinces.[20] Few demurred from Krzaklewski's judgement that all sides, as well as Poland, had suffered a defeat over the referendum.

John Paul's fifth papal visit was delayed into early June so that it would not clash with the referendum. Although he still attracted audiences of millions to hear his homilies the visit was almost entirely pastoral, compared to those of 1979, 1983, 1987 and 1991, and had little direct political effect. The left protested against the AWS's linkage of its electoral symbol to a widely distributed poster advertising his visit; overall though, the frail and sickly 77 year-old Pontiff transmitted a spiritual message designed to reverse the church's declining influence in an age when his popularity was beginning to be challenged by the likes of Michael Jackson who had just performed in Warsaw. The effect of this attempt to reinforce the church's popular character and membership base against the post-1989 pressures of secularisation and modernism remains to be seen.

The Lustration Law passed by the Sejm in April finally emerged in a sharper opposition form than Kwaśniewski's original proposal. All persons standing for high state office, as well as judges, procurators and heads of the public media, were to submit a declaration concerning their collaboration with the security agencies, including Intelligence and Counter-Intelligence, during the 1945–90 period. While such an admission would not involve automatic disqualification the truth of its contents would be checked by a newly established Lustration Court which could punish a false declaration with a ten year ban on public office holding. Kwaśniewski's signing of the law, along with Belka's economic liberalism and the constitutional capping of public debt at 60% of GDP, were interpreted as steps in his long-term aim of achieving a Historic Compromise with the UP and part of the UW. To facilitate the formation of any new coalition arrangements which might be necessitated by the results of the election of 21 September 1997 he distanced himself from Oleksy's and Miller's SdRP hardline or 'concrete' (*beton*) faction which opposed the Lustration Law.

THE ANTI-COMMUNIST CAMP MAKES A COMEBACK

A noted English journalist, Christopher Bobinski, described 1997 as 'a year of historic choices and significant hurdles'. He felt that the economic feel-good factor and the greater national security provided by imminent NATO membership would not be sufficient to ensure the SdRP's electoral success nor would the UW and the PSL necessarily hold their votes. He doubted whether Poland's politicians would assuage the bitter historical party and personal splits which remained and which he considered were still more important than actual policy divisions; he conceded that 'the old "left-right" labels make little sense any more as the political parties seek to build new identities' but took too sanguine a view of the merits of the AWS and ROP alternatives.[21] The electoral campaign started anaemically but was overshadowed by the unprecedented scale of catastrophic floods in July. There had been serious flooding in Bielsko Biała the previous September and the state of the Vistula and the Oder had given concern for over two decades. The Oder floods now killed about 50 people and affected 8 southern provinces very seriously, submerging about 50 towns and 300 villages, notably Wrocław and Opole. Politically, the delayed and insufficient assistance by the state and army, and the bureaucratic and insensitive response by the government, provided the opposition with a providential stick with which to belabour the government. But it also demonstrated dramatically the general post-communist weakness of the civil and local infrastructure of the Polish state and the vast amount of work which needed to be made up during the coming decade.

A Pentor poll in May 1997 showed that 26% intended to vote for the SLD, 25% for the AWS, 16% for the PSL, 13% for the UW, 8% for the UP, 7% for

ROP and 4% (later rising to 7%) for the Pensioners Party (KPEiR).[22] The most popular politicians were in order Zych, Kuroń, Kwaśniewski, Mazowiecki, Cimoszewicz and Olechowski followed by Balcerowicz, Pawlak, Rosati, Olszewski, Miller, Krzaklewski, Geremek and Bugaj who had more opponents than supporters. Cimoszewicz' support plummeted 12 points by August as a result of his poor handling of the floods. The Polish electorate, however, remained badly divided as to its preferred coalition after the election: 27% wanted SLD–PSL, 16% SLD–UP–UW, 15% AWS–PSL–ROP, 11% AWS–ROP, 10% AWS–ROP–UW, 8% SLD–UW and only 7% the eventual AWS–UW outcome.[23] 6,433 candidates stood for the Sejm with the support of 22 electoral and 571 provincial committees while 520 candidates were presented for the Senate on 137 lists. Turnout was low at 47.93% with 3.88% spoilt votes.

Sejm election of 21 September 1997 (Monitor Polski, No 64, 30 September 1997).

	Total Vote	% of vote	Total seats
Solidarity Electoral Action	4,427,373	33.83	202
Union of Democratic Left (SLD)	3,551,224	27.13	164
Freedom Union (UW)	1,749,518	13.37	60
Polish Peasant Party (PSL)	956,184	7.31	27
Movement for Rebuilding Poland (ROP)	727,027	5.56	5
German Minority (6 provincial lists)	79,963	0.67	2
Labour Union (UP)	620,611	4.74	0
Pensioners Party (KPEiR)	284,826	2.18	0
Union of Republican Right (UPR)	266,317	2.03	0
Bloc for Poland—National Christian Democracy	178,395	1.36	0
Pensioners Agreement (KPEiR)	212,826	1.63	0

The decisive losers in this election were the UP which failed to qualify and the PSL which lost 105 seats. The latter had discredited itself even further, in a forlorn attempt to distance itself from the SLD, by leaving the government just before the election. Pawlak was quickly replaced by Kalinowski as PSL chairman, Zych left his PSL post while UP leader Bugaj also stood down. ROP fell far short of its inflated ambitions while division into two competing parties lost the pensioners their chance of reaching the electoral threshold. The AWS won because it distanced the

SLD by 6.7% while the UW gained a markedly better result than its pre-decessors. The AWS and UW with 47.2% of the vote together gained 262 seats (almost 57%). The SLD while losing 7 seats increased its vote by 6.7%. Although it did badly in Warsaw, Gdańsk and Kraków it consoli-dated its hold over dynamic and modernising northern and western Poland. It ran out top in Bydgoszcz, Toruń and Szczecin and, more unex-pectedly, in Poznań as well. Overall the percentage of wasted or unrepre-sented votes decreased significantly to 12.13% compared to 34.43% in 1993. In the Senate election, because of electoral alliances on the right and centre, AWS won a majority with 51 seats, the UW gained 8, ROP 5, the SLD 28, PSL 3 and independents 5.

Krzaklewski remained outside the government in order to prepare for his highly likely presidential bid in 2000. Forming the new AWS-UW govern-ment led by, the politically unknown, professor, Jerzy Buzek, with Balcerow-icz as deputy-prime minister and finance minister, Geremek as foreign minister, Suchocka at Justice and Onyszkiewicz at Defense, proved a fraught process which did not bode well either for its future unity or effectiveness. It took over a month to agree a balance between the new majority's reform and preservationist wings. It was generally agreed that an enormous task faced the new government in the pressing need to reform key sectors such as local government, pensions, social security and the health service; the bulk of heavy industry and agriculture also had to be restructured ahead of EU entry while privatisation needed to be accelerated.

CONSTITUTION-MAKING AND POLITICAL INSTITUTIONS

Constitutions have always had great symbolic importance in Poland's history and in the national consciousness.[24] Progressive documents like those of 3 May 1791 and 17 March 1921 contrast with the April 1935 authoritarian draft. The Stalinist constitution of 22 July 1952, which replaced the transi-tional 'Little Constitution' of 1947, was amended on numerous occasions, most notably in 1976. The purely negotiated, evolutionary and legal-parliamentary abdication of communist power was given constitutional form in two amendments in April and December 1989: the former implemented the freedoms and established the new institutions agreed to at the Round Table; the latter abolished the PZPR's leading-role, began the shift from social to liberal political freedoms and away from economic planning, set up the Polish Republic in place of the PRL and restored the crown to the head of the eagle in the national coat of arms [Sokolewicz in Sanford 1992]. Altogether 6 such *ad hoc* changes confirmed the Rule of Law and constitutionality on the basis of a pragmatic, if muddled, separation of the powers in the initial transformation stage.

There was universal agreement on the need to replace the 1952 constitution in both the Sejm and the Senate Special Commissions on redrafting the constitution established in early 1990. But it soon became clear that there was enormous division on both the general principles and the institutional-political balances that should be written into the new document. In particular the 1991 disputes between Wałęsa and the Sejm did little to clarify the basic issues of ministerial countersignature, dissolution, legislative initiative and decree-powers. The political fragmentation confirmed by the 1991 election highlighted the vast gap between the two theoretical extremes mirroring Poland's interwar oscillation: advocates of a strong executive presidency and rationalised parliamentarianism on Gaullist lines could not be reconciled with the proponents of a cabinet-parliamentary system with the president as a figurehead Head of State.[25]

The Suchocka government, however, compromised sufficiently with Wałęsa in order to produce a transitional 'Little Constitution'. This was passed by more than the required two thirds majority on a minimum 50% vote, in the Sejm on 1 August 1992. Its partial character is reflected in its title—'The Constitutional Act on the mutual relations between the legislative and the executive institutions of the Republic of Poland and on local self-government'.[26] At best it merely confirmed the mixed and hybrid semi-presidential-parliamentary system by defining some contentious aspects such as dissolution, legislative initiative, a complicated shared procedure for cabinet formation and presidential appointment of the Chief of Staff and other military posts. As in the Fifth French Republic the dominant presidential sphere includes foreign policy and national security questions and the nomination of relevant ministers. On the other hand the president now became subject to ministerial counter-signature in the remaining fields with some exclusions. The provisional and partial character of this new institutional framework was pointed up by the appointment of a new joint parliamentary Constitutional Commission which started work on the full basic law in November 1992.

As we have seen, Wałęsa had his most bitter constitutional conflicts with the contractual Sejm at the end of its life and with Olszewski while he worked quite well with Suchocka and Pawlak. The stresses of political cohabitation diminished with Kwaśniewski's election as president; but he was also concerned to maintain a wider Head of State, rather than a sectarian SLD appeal. This aspect strengthened in 1997, especially in his support for the passing of the new constitution and his attempts to have the Concordat ratified as part of a general ideological-systemic settlement. The role of political institutions and their mutual relationships and a settled legal framework thus crystallised in this period.[27] Parliamentary life, in particular, assumed a settled institutional form although there is insufficient space to go into detail on this aspect.[28] Something like a professional and non-ideological political elite with settled procedures emerged within this framework.[29]

The above facilitated the work of the Constitutional Commission which proceeded at a leisurely pace between 1993 and 1997. In the end it had to choose between half a dozen alternative drafts and variants. The final compromise reflected the lumping together of the SLD–PSL coalition with the UP and UW drafts to protect secularism, social values and liberal citizenhood while paying due obeisance to Catholic susceptibilities. It is, consequently, a long, verbose and unpolished document of 243 articles, grouped under 13 different chapter headings.[30] Contradictory aims and statements are lumped together in what the French call a *négre-blanche* way while their resolution is left to future political practice; the state's unitary character (article 3) is balanced by a commitment to decentralisation (article 15), the protection of the family farm (article 23) stands alongside free market and inheritance rights (articles 21–22) and so on. Challenged by the populist nationalism and integral Catholicism of the right and of significant sections of the AWS alliance the constitution remained a political football reflecting residual Polish conflicts over values and traditions just as much as differing conceptions of society and economy. But its dominant features were the classical liberal ones of democracy, rule of law, national sovereignty, protection of almost every type of right and the post-communist leftist and Catholic commitment to implementing 'the principles of social justice' (article 2) for 'the common good of all its citizens' (article 1).

The long-drawn out process of writing the constitution, the Catholic-secular dispute and the political divisions ahead of the September 1997 parliamentary elections explain why the Polish electorate viewed it with so little enthusiasm. They barely passed it on a low turnout in the referendum. A poll showed that 42% thought that it would be subject to further revision fairly quickly. But this was an unfair judgement. Apart from detail little adjustment took place in the political mechanisms and institutional balances inherited from the 'Little Constitution' on which something like an elite concensus had emerged. As well as accepting the semi-presidential-parliamentary system it confirmed anew the important role of a highly differentiated judicial sector with growing powers of judicial review developing the principle of the separation of the powers.[31] Such bodies as the constitutional tribunal, the state tribunal and the Spokesman for Citizens' Rights had emerged in the 1980s alongside the older branches of criminal, civil, labour and administrative courts. The Poles have a developed tendency for codification, adopted from both Napoleonic and German sources: a major revision of the Criminal and Criminal Procedure Codes (abolishing the death penalty) was completed in 1997. The transitional stage of democratisation thus saw an uneasy co-existence between older *Rechtsstaat* concepts and those of popular sovereignty linked with some decline in presidential power.

POLITICAL PARTIES AND ISSUES

The PZPR dominated what Jerzy Wiatr has called a 'hegemonic party-system' with the minor United Peasant Party (ZSL) and Democratic Party (SD) during the communist period.[32] This allowed for more pluralism and even marginal opposition from catholic groupings notably *Znak* (the Sign) and its successors, than in other communist systems. The Round Table con-tract, in effect, polarised parliamentary and party political life into two camps, the Solidarity conglomerate and the communist and allied grouping in 1989. Both split very quickly. Solidarity divided over its presidential can-didates in 1990. Mazowiecki's wing turned into ROAD and then the Demo-cratic Union (UD).[33] Wałęsa benefitted from the support of the Centre Alliance but he quarrelled with the Kaczyński twins and refused to allow them to build up the Centre Party (PC) as a Gaullist type of electoral force. The PZPR dissolved itself in January 1990. Its long-term successor, the Social Democracy of the Polish Republic (SdRP), established itself as a major force and ensured the successful continuation of this tradition.[34]

The inauguration of democratic freedoms of political life and organisation saw an explosion in the number of parties who legally registered their stat-utes into three figures; the number rose to 222 by July 1993 and about 330 by Summer 1997 when the extremely liberal 1990 registration law was tight-ened up. Many were small local or sectional groups, hardly more than pres-sure groups, with minimal membership and weak organisation, hence the dismissal of the bulk of them as 'sofa-parties'. The crucial factor was the gain-ing of parliamentary representation but the simplification of the party system was complicated by a large number of cross-cutting cleavages. The peasant, right and centre parts of the electorate from 1991 onwards have been particu-larly fissiparous as personalities and parties produced recurring multiple challenges using a variety of labels for the same electoral ground.

We have already noted that the founding election of the new democratic order took a contractual form in Poland in 1989 while the first fully free elec-tion in 1991 resulted in a great degree of fragmentation. Sartori has pointed to the crucial importance of the timing of the introduction of a free and complete franchise and of proportional representation. The dynamics of democratic politics are subsequently determined by the number and structure of cleavages as well as the degree of party organisation.[35] On the other hand Gebethner has shown that the Sejm in Poland's intermediate transition stage from 1991–1993 did no more than reflect the country's divisions which would have occurred irrespective of proportional representation.[36] The real causes were the immature process of party aggregation, the intensity and number of varied divisions and the confusion introduced by Wałęsa's destabilising role as president. That the two most successful parties only held 12% of the seats apiece and that ten had Sejm representation into double figures certainly placed 1991–93 Poland at the extreme end of multi-partyism. But the Suchocka experience showed that this could be reconciled with effective democratic government based on coalition-building. The 1993 result, on the other hand, demonstrated the simplifying benefits of minimum electoral thresholds at the price of excluding about a third of the electorate from any Sejm representation.

A major Polish work on political parties identifies no less than 16 major streams plus another six minor ones.[37] Taxonomies based on historical traditions or origins do not, however, take us very far. What is striking is the relative failure of interwar parties to make significant comebacks. The PPS label and tradition, broke up into numerous quarrelsome factions before being digested by the SLD, the UP and UW after 1993. The PSL—Polish Peasant Party—strand has survived, but in terms of personel it seems to have much more continuity with the ZSL of the communist period. Many of the Christian–democratic, conservative, Catholic and nationalist parties have gone back to interwar labels and invoked symbols and traditions dating from this period but this has not helped them to establish themselves. The SdRP and the PSL are more clearly direct successor-parties to the PZPR and the ZSL of the communist period. The SD vanished from the scene along with pro-communist regime Catholic formations such as PAX and the more independent Christian-Social Union. The issues of the PZPR inheritance and funds have periodically been raised by its opponents to trip up the SdRP. A favourable repayment agreement was negotiated by the latter with the State Treasury just before the Cimoszewicz government left office.

The dominant historical division remains that between Solidarity and the camp of successors to communism which took shape from 1988 onwards. Although it is fading this still explains the emotional animosity felt by the UW, large parts of the UP and the SL/PL sections of the peasant parties, all of which have developed out of the Solidarity camp, against successor-communists.

Personal and historical hatreds and experiences, such as martial law internment, 1980s opposition, the Solidarity–OPPZ rivalry and incomplete victory in 1989–93 are thus usually more potent forces for division than agreement. Unity on individual policy issues against conservative, nationalist and Catholic rivals, however, came into increasing play on constitutional, religious and socioeconomic questions after Kwaśniewski's election.

One can follow Tomasz Żukowski in identifying a spectrum made up of the following four sets of cleavages in contemporary Poland which complicates the simple left-right political categorisation: 1) the catholic-secular, 2) the economic, ranging from market liberalism to social market and state interventionist forms, 3) the nationalist, which used to be defined in terms of regaining sovereignty from Soviet control but which is nowadays expressed in terms of defending traditional Polish values as well as in attitudes towards European Union and minorities, 4) the historic Solidarity-communist conflict.[38] The simplification of the party system was reflected in the decline of political clubs in the Sejm from 18 during 1989–91 to 11 plus 6 circles in 1991–93, 6 clubs in 1993–97 and 4 clubs post-1997. By the mid-1990s there were still about two dozen significant national parties but they could, in essence, be reduced to seven ideological streams.[39]: 1) Socialist (UP/PPS), 2) Social-Democrat (SLD/SdRP), 3) Peasant (PSL and Radical-Peasant Party, LR), 4) Populist (Solidarity, KPN and BBWR), 5) Liberal (UW), 6) Conservative-Liberal (Aleksander Hall's Conservative Party PK, Paweł Łączkowski's Christian-Democratic Party PChD, Janus Korwin-Mikke's Union of Real Politics UPR, Józef Ślisz's Christian-Peasant Party SLCh), 7) The even more fragmented National-Catholic stream was made of two groupings, a) Polish Friendship made up of 5 parties (Chrzanowki's ZChN, Kaczyński's PC, Gabriel Janowski's Peasant Alliance PL, Romuald Szeremietiew's Movement for the Republic RdR, Michał Ujazdowski's Conservative Coalition KK) and b) the four party Centre-Right Secretariat Grouping (Jan Parys' Movement for the Third Republic RTR, Andrzej Anusz' Polish Union ZP, Wojciech Ziembiński's Party of Fidelity to the Republic SWR, Tadeusz Jackowski's ChD-SP).

The most significant step well ahead of the September 1997 election was the emergence of the Solidarity 'Election Action' (AWS) with Marian Krzaklewski as chairman. Its co-ordinating committee elected in April 1997 marked a move towards the anti-European, nationalist and Catholic radical right where it competed for the same ground as Olszewski's Movement for Rebuilding Poland (ROP) although they made a significant electoral pact for the 1997 Senate elections. Krzaklewski's four vice-chairmen represented the ZChN, KPN, Federation of Associations of Catholic Families and Solidarity, while 7 of the remaining seats went to Solidarity along with representation for the PSL–PL, Lech Wałęsa Institute, Christian Democratic Party (PCD), Conservative–Peasant Party (SK–L), Centre Party (PC), Andrzej Olechowski's Movement of One Hundred (RS), Romuald Szeremietiew's Movement for the Republic (RdR–OP) and Andrzej Anusz' New Poland. Much of AWS's support came from manual workers and the unemployed which explains its populist attacks against the alleged collaboration of the UW and the UP with the successor-communist SLD and PSL.

One of the most important questions currently being debated is the extent to which the SdRP has been 'social-democratised'.[40] We have noted that by 1997 little distinguished the SdRP in ideological and policy terms from the UP and that it shares civic-liberal values with the UW. The differentiating factor is largely structural, the organisational and membership continuity with the old PZPR and the emotional split perpetuated by the memory of Solidarity-communist divisions. One of the key issues at the time of the September 1997 election was whether its results would encourage the renovating strand within the SLD/SdRP led by Kwaśniewski and Cimoszewicz to bridge the gap with sections of the UP, the UW, the peasant parties and even Solidarity; in the event the emergence of a clear AWS–UW majority and coalition government favoured the resurgence of the vocabulary of ideological-historically based confrontation between the successors to the 1989 communist and anti-communist camps. This was a smokescreen for sections of the AWS which wanted to protect their electoral and trade union constituencies from the marketisation costs of the systemic transformation in exchange for greater democratisation defined as a purge of pre-1989 office-holders. However, apart from minority and technician governments the only alternatives to the Buzek AWS–UW majority in the Sejm elected in September 1997, was an AWS–SLD Great Coalition or the restructuring of both the AWS and the SLD favoured by Kwaśniewski. The latter would bridge the existing party gap by creating cross-cutting alliances of common social and economic policies which would heal the historical animosities of 1989. In this way a modern left and a modern right would emerge in Poland but the historical experience of such countries as Ireland and Italy suggest that this desirable outcome is most unlikely.

If political coalitions were diverse internal political coalescence was also incomplete and parties were still divided by competing ideological and personal factions despite low membership, only the 1993 figures of 200,000 for the PSL, 65,000 for the SdRP, 35,000 for the KPN and 15–20,000 for the UW being significantly large.[41] The UW was torn between Jan Rokita's catholic–liberal (until it left), Frasyniuk's liberal and Zofia Kuratowska's social–liberal tendencies. The SdRP was likewise rent by the internal controversies between Kwaśniewski's and Cimoszewicz's social–liberal stance, the residual marxist socialism of Leszek Miller's tendency and Oleksy's post-apparat stream. The former found some support within the UP although the majority went along with Bugaj's harder socialist line which established more common ground with the successor-communists. The SLD alliance was, in turn, tested by OPZZ and national teachers' union demands. Given their membership and organisational weakness and criticism of party links with business it is hardly surprising that the new 1997 law on political parties laid down the state funding of parties which gained parliamentary representation.

THE DYNAMICS OF TRANSFORMATION

The only safe prediction about Polish politics is that events move rapidly, often but not invariably cyclically, and that they are normally difficult to predict. Lijphart adapted Rokkan's 'freezing' thesis in 1992 to postulate that 1989 power-sharing inevitably led to Poland's subsequent constitutional choices;[42] proportional representation and a dual executive in which a directly elected president with considerable prerogatives shares power with a prime minister answerable to parliament. Democratic consolidation, however, increases public confidence in political alternation. This, along with the simplification of the party system, has weakened the need for electoral and institutional mechanisms to ensure pluralistic power-sharing with the consequences which we have seen from 1993 onwards. The strong presidency may weaken, as in France, and much depended upon the nature of Kwaśniewski's cohabitation with the post-1997 AWS–UW parliamentary majority; but only a full-blooded crisis would shift Poland towards a cabinet-parliamentary system with a weak head of state type of presidency as in Hungary. We shall, therefore, consider in the following chapter whether Poland's continuing socio-economic transformation and the clash between modernisation and its traditional political values still holds the possibility of future political explosions or whether the system has bedded down in essentials.

1 Jadwiga Staniszkis, *The Dynamics of the Breakthrough. The Polish Experience* (Berkeley: University of California Press, 1991). Unattributed public opinion polls in the remaining chapters are drawn from *Wprost*.

2 Michael Mandelbaum (ed), *Post-Communism. Four Perspectives* (New York: Council on Foreign Relations, 1996).

3 George Sanford, 'Communism's weakest link—democratic capitalism's greatest challenge' in G. Pridham, E. Herring & G. Sanford (eds), *Building Democracy. The International dimension of Democratisation in Eastern Europe* (Leicester: Leicester UP, 2nd. edn 1997).

4   Walter Connor & Piotr Płoszajski (eds), *The Polish Road from Socialism* (Armonk NY: M.E. Sharpe, 1992). The reports on attitudes and values during the 1980s in the *Poles* series published by the Institute of Philosophy and Sociology (IFIS) of the Polish Academy of Sciences (PAN) provides an unrivalled primary source; cf. *Polacy 90'* (Warsaw: IFIS–PAN, 1991).

5   Wiktor Osiatyński in Jon Elster (ed), *The Roundtable Talks and the Breakdown of Communism* (Chicago: University of Chicago Press, 1996), p. 21.

6   Krzysztof Dubiński (ed), *Magdalenka. Transakcja Epoki*. (Warsaw: BGW, 1990).

7   *Porozumienia Okrągłego Stołu* (Warsaw: 5 April 1989).

8   Paul Lewis, 'Non-competitive elections and regime-change: Poland 1989', *Parliamentary Affairs*, vol 43, no 1 (January 1990), pp. 90–107.

9   The insider's critique of these flaws by Jarosław Kurski has never been refuted, only sidestepped, *Lech Wałęsa. Democrat or Dictator* (Boulder, CO: Westview, 1993). Sympathetic western academic accounts tend to underestimate the influence of Wałęsa's advisers in keeping him on the rails. Cf. Voytek Zubek, 'Wałęsa's leadership and Poland's transformation', *Problems of Communism*, vol 40, no 1–2 (1991), pp. 69–83

10 *Polityka*, 8 December 1990. Stanisław Gebethner & Kryzysztof Jasiewicz, *Dlaczego tak głosowano. Wybory prezydenckie 90'* (Warsaw: ISP PAN, 1993).

11 D. Mason, D. Nelson & B. Szlarski, ' Apathy and the birth of democracy: the Polish Struggle', *East European Politics and Societies*, vol 5, no 2 (Spring 1991).

12 Stanisław Gebethner & Jacek Raciborski, *Wybory 91' a polska scena polityczna* (Warsaw: INP UW, 1992). George Sanford, 'Delay and Disappointment: the Fully Free Polish Election of 27 October 1991', *Journal of Communist Studies*, vol 9, no 2 (June 1993), pp. pp. 107–18. Tomasz Żukowski, 'Wybory parlamentarne 91', *Studia Polityczne*, vol 1, no 1 (1992), pp. 35–60.

13 Krzysztof Jasiewicz, 'From Solidarity to Fragmentation', *Journal of Democracy*, vol 3, no 2 (April 1992), pp. 55–69.

14 Frances Millard,'The Polish Parliamentary Elections of October 1991', *Soviet Studies*, vol 44, no 5 (1992), p. 853.

15 Kenneth Ka-Lok Chan, 'Poland at the Crossroads: the 1993 General Election', *Soviet Studies*, vol 47, no 1 (1995), pp. 123–45.

16 Frances Millard, 'The 1995 Polish Presidential Election', *Journal of Communist Studies and Transitional Politics*, vol 12, no 1 (March 1996), pp. 101–109.

17 *Polityka*, 4 May 1996, p.17.

18 *Biała Księga. Akta śledztwa prowadzonego przez Prokuraturę Warszawskiego Okręgu Wojskowego w Warszawie w sprawie wniosków Ministra Spraw Wewnętrznych z dnia 19.12.1995 r. I 16. 01.1996 r.* (Warsaw: Centrum Informacyjne Rządu, 1996).

19 *Polityka*, 18 May 1996, pp. 20–25.

20 *Gazeta Wyborcza*, 27 May 1997.

21 *Financial Times*, 26 March 1997.

22 *Wprost*, 4 May 1997, pp. 26–28.

23 *Wprost*, 29 June 1997, p. 23.

24 Andrzej Ajnenkiel, *Polskie konstytucje* (Warsaw: Wyd. Szkolne i Pedagogiczne, 1991).

25 Wojciech Sokolewicz, 'The Polish Constitution in a Time of Change', *International Journal of the Sociology of Law,* vol 20 (1992), pp. 29–42. Kenneth Thompson (ed), *Poland in a World of Change. Constitutions, Presidents and Politics* (Lanham MD: University Press of America, 1992).

26 Warsaw: Sejm Publishing Office, 1993.

27 *Prawo w okresie przemian ustrojowych w Polsce* (Warsaw: INP PAN-Scholar, 1995).

28 Paweł Sarnecki, *Senat RP a Sejm i Zgromadzenie Narodowe* (Warsaw: Wyd. Sejmowe, 1995). Maurice Simon, 'Institutional development of Poland's post-communist Sejm', *Journal of Legislative Studies*, vol 2, no 1 (Spring 1996), pp. 60–81.

29 For the residual divisions within it see Włodzimierz Wesołowski & Irena Panków (eds), *Świat elity politycznej* (Warsaw: IFIS PAN, 1995).

30 *The Constitution of the Republic of Poland* (Warsaw: Sejm Chancellory, 1997).

31 Wojciech Sokolewicz, 'The principle of the separation of the powers in law and constitutional jurisprudence of the Republic of Poland', *Polish Contemporary Law*, no 1–4/109–112 (1996), pp. 17–31.

32 Jerzy Wiatr in E. Allardt & Y. Littunen (eds), *Cleavages, Ideologies and Party Systems* (Helsinki: Westermarck, 1964).

33 On differentiation within the post-Solidarity camp see Mirosława Grabowska & Tadeusz Szawiel, *Anatomia elit politycznych. Partie polityczne w post-komunistycznej Polsce 1991–93* (Warsaw: IS UW, 1993).

34 George Sanford, 'Poland' in Bogdan Szajkowski (ed), *New Political Parties of Eastern Europe and the Soviet Union* (Harlow UK; Longman, 1991).

35 Giovani Sartori, *Parties and Party-Systems* (Cambridge: CUP, 1976).

36 Stanisław Gebethner, 'Mitologia złej ordynacji', *Nowa Europa*, 30 April–2 May 1992.

37 Małgorzata Dehnel-Szyc & Jadwiga Stachura, *Gry Polityczne. Orientacje na Dziś* (Warsaw: Volumen, 1991).

38 *Polityka*, 10 July 1993, p. 15.

39 *Wprost*, 15 May 1994, pp. 19–20.

40 Cf. M. Waller, B. Coppieters & K. Deschouwer (eds), *Social Democracy in Post-Communist Europe* (Ilford UK: Frank Cass, 1994).

41 Paul Lewis, 'Poland and Eastern Europe', *Democratization*, vol 2, no 1 (1995), p. 104.

42 Arend Lijphart in *Sisyphus Social Studies*, vol 1 (no viii, 1992), pp. 87–102.

Chapter 3

ECONOMY, SOCIETY AND MODERNISATION

Wiktor Herer and Władysław Sadowski argue that modern Poland has been marked by a basic contradiction between a European culture and a backward economy [Gomulka & Polonsky 1990, ch. 6]. They discern what they term a Byzantine model in which wholly authoritarian leadership patterns are coupled with irresponsible social behaviour especially bad labour discipline and productivity. On the other hand the Prussian model in East Germany, Czechoslovakia and the Poznań and Silesian parts of Poland combined an efficient bureaucratic state with social habits of obedience and organisation. Interwar Poland with 63% of its workforce in agriculture, much of it rotting away unproductively, and its most profitable industry run by foreign capital was habitually referred to as 'Europe B'. But its educational, rail, postal, state institutions and much of its urban, not to mention its vibrant intellectual and cultural life was on a European level; this made the contrast with its backward sectors even more striking. Interwar Poland combined professional and skilled working classes on European or Czech levels of efficiency, remuneration and behaviour with Third World levels of backwardness in rural southern and eastern Poland. This explains why postwar governments benefitted not only from genuine popular enthusiasm for socio-economic reconstruction but also from the desire to break out of the constraints of the backward and peripheral form of capitalism of the time; the latter cannot sensibly be compared with its dynamic contemporary successor.

It took time for the costs of the imposed Soviet economic planning and command system and of the priority of forced industrialisation after 1948 to become evident.[1] But one should remember two crucial factors. Firstly, the Soviet system was never fully established. The 1956 upheaval, which included the June 1956 Poznań uprising sparked off by industrial worker discontent, left 80% of the land in private hands, a significant small trade and retailing sector and weak state control which allowed an increasingly important black market to flourish.[2] Secondly, the communist leaders were forced into repeated political compromises with Polish society from 1956 onwards which allowed much pluralism and, even more, ambiguous confusion. The totalitarian drive of 1948–54 was replaced by an authoritarian system which adopted a variety of domesticist, nationalist, consumerist and corporatist policies in order to survive. Various sectional and only partially completed reforms also contributed to the emergence of an eclectic and hybrid mixed model. Western political scientists were, therefore, often as inclined to compare Poland's development and potential with Mexico as with the more orthodox communist states.

On the other hand the hard core of the Soviet system of communist party monopoly rule and industrial development and management established by Stalinism proved very difficult to reform, let alone dismantle.[3] The system had vast modernisation achievements to its credit. These can be confirmed by the economic growth, industrialisation, urbanisation educational, health and other statistics of the quarter of a century after the Second World War.[4] The evidence is mixed and inconclusive as to whether alternative forms of capitalist and democratic development were available at that time; the postwar experience tends to disprove it. The pre-1974 Iberian and Greek experience also shows the long gestation period necessary for economic take-off very starkly. On the other hand specialists from Huntington onwards have long conceded that communism, despite its social and economic inefficiencies was a specific form of modernisation.[5]

What is clear is that Gierek's dash for growth and consumerism in the early 1970s, based on large-scale financial and technological lending from the West, had the right strategic aims but was mismanaged in practice. The result was an unparalled economic collapse starting in 1978 which had dramatic political repercussions. Estimated year on decline in GNP was 2.3% in 1979, 6% in 1980, 12% in 1981 and 5% in 1982 representing a fall of over a quarter between 1978 to 1982. The Solidarity explosion in 1980 was controlled by martial law which allowed the system to limp on until 1989. The agenda then became one of systemic-replacement and the shift towards a modern society, what Karl Polanyi calls the 'great transformation' rather than one of internal reform.[6]

One school of thought blames Gierek's mistakes but this is hardly convincing given the bloc-wide collapse of communism. The case for the systemic exhaustion of the command-directive system of real or actually existing socialism is, therefore, conclusive.[7] The communist system just could not cope with the required shift in the 1970s from an extensive to an intensive model of development. More seriously the civic, cultural and social behaviour of the Poles was such that once terror was abandoned Western norms and expectations in terms of life-styles and consumer patterns became predominant. The system faced a distribution crisis because its egalitarian ideology was contradicted by everyday shortages and injustices which were blamed on the communist controlled state not on market allocation. The result was that attempts to impose economic restructuring through financial austerity and price-rises triggered of social explosions in 1970, 1976 and 1980.[8]

Criticism of elite corruption and demands for greater equality and intra-systemic socialist renewal quickly led to political demands for power-sharing especially for free trade unions and factory self-management which the regime found unacceptable. The mixture of economic failure and superficial repression then led on to root-and-branch systemic rejection. The failure of the communist system to achieve Western consumerism and life-styles sparked off the historical Polish propensity for society to coalesce against a hostile state.[9] In this way rejection of the Soviet form of Byzantine model for both cultural and efficiency reasons was matched by a full acceptance of the Return to Europe which initially was equated, uncritically, with democratic capitalism.

Jaruzelski's partially successful consultative and economic reform responses, however, continued the internal transformation of the system and ensured that its ending would take an evolutionary and politically non-violent form.[10] Bartołomiej Kamiński has also argued that Polish communism managed its systemic decline very effectively and that this set important constraints on marketisation initially.[11] A revealing statistic is that 4.9 million out of a workforce of 17.2 million worked officially in the private sector in 1986 (admittedly 3.8 million in agriculture) producing a quarter of GDP; one can also estimate that a further 600,000 worked in some sort of black or other coloured market.[12] The Messner government encouraged the establishment of Polonia firms run by Poles abroad and a 1987 law made it possible for state enterprises to transform themselves into joint-stock companies. It also took measures in the form of leasing or sale to insiders within the communist establishment which favoured the growth of what came to be called *nomenklatura* capitalism.[13]

TOWARDS THE MARKET SOCIETY

Poland suffered two main economic shocks after 1989, the first linked with Balcerowicz's stabilisation and the second caused by the collapse of Soviet and communist bloc trade in 1991. As a result of prime minister Rakowski's freeing of prices the budget deficit increased 16-fold during 1989, retail prices went up by 244% while the money supply quadrupled.[14] Leszek Balcerowicz, the deputy-prime minister for the economy and minister of finance in Mazowiecki's government, therefore, had to achieve financial stabilisation to control this hyper-inflation and to combine this with the liberalisation and de-monopolisation associated with the shift from a command to a market economy. Advised by the Harvard economist Jeffrey Sachs, Balcerowicz rejected a cautious and prepared sequencing of the economic transition.[15]

He adopted a neo-liberal 'big-bang' strategy in his comprehensive plan for shock-therapy which rejected more gradualist social democratic approaches.[16] The domestic freeing and convertibility of the *złoty*, huge interest rate rises and savage cuts to decrease the state budget deficit achieved an acceptable degree of stabilisation by bringing inflation down to well under three figures. At the same time foreign and domestic trade and economic activity were liberalised through deregulation and the initial privatisation of the small industry and retailing sectors.[17] The development of a new legal-financial framework emerged in a more evolutionary manner. Legal regulations were changed piecemeal, a stock-exchange was established in 1991 and new financial institutions and practices developed. Political life was dominated during 1990–94 by the debate on the safety net which Poland could afford in terms of unemployment and social welfare benefits during the transition period. *Złoty* devaluation also produced a large trade surplus with the Comecon countries in 1990. All this gained the support of the IMF and World Bank who promised aid worth $2.5 billion despite the suspension of debt-servicing.

Financial policy was, however, much less successful subsequently, partly because of the political confusion of the Bielecki and Olszewski periods. The collapse of exports by about 40–60% following the shift to hard currency trading with the ex-Comecon countries in 1991 was aggravated by the increased cost of imports especially Russian oil and gas.[18] The social and political consequences were that Balcerowicz's successful stabilisation and initial shift to the market during 1989–91 was bought at the price of heavy economic recession and real falls in the standard of living causing the pauperisation of much of the population. GDP fell by 9% in 1991 (the public sector by 19% compared to a 25% increase in the private sector) while a large budget deficit and 74% inflation provoked the strikewave of Summer 1991. Jerzy Eysymontt attempted some economic reflation under Olszewski but did not modify Balcerowicz's framework significantly if only because of the need to maintain international confidence. Suchocka, on the other hand dealt with industrial discontent by producing a corporatist 'Social Pact' for state-industry which involved the OPZZ and the Solidarity TU directly in enterprise management and privatisation. The economic recovery which started in 1992 and built-up subsequently came too late to save the Solidarity and anti-communist camp electorally but by then the most painful period of transformation had passed. The decline in Polish GDP of 17% from 1989–92 was, however, the same as Hungary's, a touch less than Slovenia, Slovakia and the Czech Republic and vastly less painful than Romania's 32% or Bulgaria's 28% collapse.

The main aims of economic restructuring were twofold; firstly, to carry out the privatisation required by the shift to market capitalism and secondly, to adjust through closure or modernisation to global competition and the need to prepare for EU entry. The former was overseen from Summer 1990 onwards by a ministry of ownership transformation. It had little difficulty in disposing rapidly of small firms and the retailing and service sector, within the confines of the 1990 privatisation law, through public auctions. A million new jobs emerged in the private sector, made up of 1.6 million firms during 1990–91, to counterbalance a corresponding shrinkage in the public sector. The former employed over 50% of the workforce by 1993, making up almost half of GDP. The figure was 65% of employment and 60% of production in 1996; by that time private firms outnumbered state ones by three to one even though 95% only employed five or less workers.

The real problem was the over 8,000 large-scale state enterprises which were to be halved in number by 1997; these were commercialised through conversion into joint-stock companies, with their shares held by the state treasury, so that they could compete on the market. Such firms were subject to the *popiwek* or surplus wage-tax which was designed to encourage them to restructure and to lessen the need for state subsidies. Much debate took place in 1990 as to the best method of privatisation which involved choosing between liquidation, managerial or employee buyout or direct sale to either a foreign or domestic buyer.[19] The liberal-dominated Mazowiecki government adopted the costly and cumbersome British type of procedure of offering firms for sale to the public individually. Apart from token gestures to works councils and employees' share-buying they also abandoned a whole decade of Solidarity rhetoric on workers' self-management. Only 668 enterprises were disposed off by the state in this way during 1990–92 while another 1,810 had begun the process.

This slow pace encouraged discussion of effecting the transfer through the distribution of vouchers or shares to all citizens as in Czecho-Slovakia. This approach was favoured by Janusz Lewandowski, Bielecki's ownership transformation minister, who produced a mass privatization programme in June 1991 based on the distribution of vouchers or free shares in 400 of the largest state enterprises and the establishment of investment funds with majority 60% private participation. The recession and political in-fighting postponed the passing of an attenuated version of Lewandowski's scheme by the Sejm until April 1993. Lewandowski had, however, missed his moment. He barely survived as a minister under Suchocka, because of the strong shift back towards social corporatism and workers' rights and against foreign capitalism. In practice, ownership empowerment of society was just another of

Wałęsa's empty slogans and was an insufficient response to growing opposition of both the OPZZ and the Solidarity trade unions, backed by the national protectionism of the KPN and ZChN, to purely managerial and capitalist forms of development. Such ambitious aims were eventually replaced by more sectional and limited programmes of privatisation, geared at attracting foreign buyers and investors. Over 93% of the agricultural land held by state farms was either sold off or leased by the Agricultural Property Agency after 1990. On the other hand although a private market developed in housing it is still very much split between the mainly rural properties which have full freehold tenure and the bulk of urban ex-housing co-operative and municipal housing which often still has only a questionable form of leasehold. The issue of property rights has, in addition, been bedevilled by the problem of restitution or compensation for owners who had property confiscated by both the Nazis and the communists. The Bielecki government accepted the principle of property restitution. The argument about the best form of compensation and whether it should largely be financial in the form of bonds held up the passing of a law to regulate the matter although a special arrangement was agreed for the Roman Catholic church in late 1991.

There had been much continuity in economic policy during 1989–93 despite the drift from the neo-liberalism of the 'big-bang' to the moderate corporatism of the enterprise pact. The very determined Balcerowicz and his associates and successors were increasingly affected by interest groups and political pressures. The political fragmentation of the time, however, allowed them to create and maintain a concensus around the post-1989 principles of stabilisation, liberalisation and restructuring. The 1993 electoral victory of the PSL–SLD was partly brought about by the feeling that the social costs of economic transformation were too heavy and needed to be phased out over a longer time-period. The left's own spokesmen also promised a move towards the German form of social market which would protect the groups which were most at risk during the transition. It was also quite obvious that the PSL was 'little more than the political wing of the agricultural lobby'.[20] Purely preservationist policies dominated the rural sector as borne out by the imposition of a tariff on food imports in Summer 1994.

In practice, as discussed in chapter 2, the result of SLD–PSL infighting, government conflicts with Wałęsa during 1993–95 over the state budget and scraps for territorial influence between the finance ministry and the National Bank headed by Gronkiewicz-Waltz all consolidated, rather than weakened, Kołodko's position. As deputy-prime minister and finance minister from May 1994 to February 1997 his 'Strategy for Poland' determined economic policy; he achieved as dominating an influence as Balcerowicz, before him.

Kołodko was fortunate that his basic assumption of an average 5% p.a. growth rate during the 1994–97 medium term was proved right. This enabled favourable growth in consumption and foreign trade as well as investment thus bringing about his golden scenario of growth-led expansion resolving social discontent. On the other hand while the inflation rate was cut to 19% by 1996 this was only half the highly optimistic single level figure which he promised because 'electoral economics' produced a wave of price increases in Autumn 1996. He also left a severe and growing trade deficit in 1997. The *popiwek* went in early 1995, after 5 years to be replaced by a tripartite commission setting ceilings on earnings in state industry and a move towards collective bargaining. Restructuring in the agricultural sector took place without much purposive government policy. The pause on privatisation in the industrial sector, although the mass privatisation programmme was offically relaunched in December 1994, continued throughout the Pawlak and Oleksy governments because of the political quagmire caused by the long-stretched out reform of the central and economic administration. The much delayed pensions and banking reforms were only introduced after Belka took over. As we have seen, the former stimulated the rise of the 'flash-party' representing pensioners concerned by the end of the automatic indexation which they had got used to in the good old communist days. Kwaśniewski and Cimoszewicz prepared for the 1997 elections with a renewed bout of privatisation in order to demonstrate their social liberal credentials and to build bridges to the UW and UP.

Overall judgements on the economic policy of the left-peasant governments of 1994–97 need to balance two considerations. On the one hand Kołodko stimulated and maintained economic growth. He achieved a degree of financial stabilisation and attenuated the social crisis of the early transition period. The budget deficit, as a percentage of GDP, was kept between 2.5 to 2.8% during his period of office. On the other hand critics argue that too much time was wasted in addressing the inevitable restructuring of key sectors such as energy, raw material extraction, tele-communications, pensions and insurance. They hoped that an energetic second bout of renewed liberalisation and restructuring would emerge as a result of the 1997 election. Unfortunately the Solidarity-national Catholic AWS contained forces which seemed even more protectionist than the PSL-Miller/Oleksy SdRP *beton* despite their anti-communist rhetoric. One could not be too hopeful that a strong reforming impetus would emerge after October1997 based on the UW–UP coalition with the tacit support of the SdRP social liberals. The Polish political elite largely shared the moderate-reform concensus so the big issue became the extent to which this might be accelerated by the externally promoted need to prepare Poland for EU entry; its negotiation, and the attendant restructuring, was bound to dominate the Warsaw political scene for the remainder of the century and would determine the final shape of the country's modernisation.

The main indicators of Poland's economic performance in the 1990s can be summarised as follows:[21]

% compared to previous year	1990	1991	1992	1993	1994	1995	1996
National Income (GDP)	−11.6	−7.4	1.5	3.8	5.2	7.0	6.0
Industry	−24.2	−11.9	4.2	5.6	13.1	10.2	8.8
Inflation	585.8	70.3	43.0	37.6	29.5	21.6	18.5
Unemployment	6.5	12.2	14.8	16.4	16.0	14.9	13.6
Real per capita income	−24.4	−0.3	−3.6	−2.9	0.5	4.6	6.1

GETTING FIT FOR EUROPE

The EU Commission 'Opinion' of July 1997 noted that while Poland's population was 11% of the EU its economy was only 3% and that its per capita GDP was 31% of the EU average. The massive 30% decline (11–12 million) in the 1938 population of 36 million to 23.6 million in 1946 and the changes in its ethnic composition at the end of the Second World War have already been discussed in Chapter 1. But a high birth rate in the 1950s and 1960s, which tailed-off into a more typical low birth-rate/low mortality European pattern, increased the number of Poles to 29.8 million in 1960, 35.7 million in 1980 and 38.609 million in 1995. It is estimated that the population will peak, and then stabilise, somewhere in the 41–43 million range by 2020. The population density increased from 76 per square kilometre in 1946 to 124 in 1995. The unfavourable ratio of 114 females to 100 males in 1946 decreased to 106 to 100 in 1995. 59.2% of the population was economically active in 1994 but the country had an ageing population. People's Poland had fairly closed frontiers apart from German and Jewish emigration until 1980. Since then about a million Poles have emigrated, many unofficially, (mainly to Germany, 61%) for labour reasons. A trickle of Third World immigration has been bolstered by a vast influx of over 2 million from the ex-USSR in the 1990s.

The main demographic features of the first half of the communist period were dominated by high rates of industrialisation and urbanisation. The percentage living in urban areas went up from 34% in 1946, 48.3% in 1960, 58.7% in 1980 to 61.8% in 1995. The share of industry in GDP increased from 19.3% in 1931, 31% in 1949 to 50.2% in 1980 but fell back to 44.9% in 1990 and 38% in 1992. Manufacturing employed 24.9% of the workforce in 1995 compared to 26.5% in agriculture, fisheries and forestry, 5.5% in building, 12.7% in services, 1.3% in hotels and restaurants, 5.6% in transport, 6.0% in education and 6.7% in the health and social services.

The macroeconomic structure of the country changed as follows between 1989 and 1993; the share of agriculture in GDP decreased from 12.9% to 6.7%, industry and building went from 52.3% to 38.6% while the service and administrative sector, in its broadest definition, rose from 34.8% to 54.7%. According to GUS statistical yearbooks the percentage employed in the private sector increased from 44.3% in 1989, to 45.1% in 1990, 50.2% in 1991, 53.7% in 1992, 56.8% in 1993, 59.4% in 1994 and 61.9% in 1995. The private sector share of GDP increased from 28.6% in 1989, 42.1% in 1991, 45.2% in 1992, 47.9% in 1993 to 46.4% in 1994. In agriculture private sector employment went from 88.2% in 1989 to 95% in 1993, in industry from 27.3% to 46.9%, in retailing and domestic trade from 9.3% to 92.5% and in building from 33.3% to 80.9% for the same years. By sector the 1994 shares were 90% in agriculture, 38% in industry (rising to 52% in 1996), 86% in building and 89% in retailing. Poland had 419,313 privately owned shops to 6,287 state owned ones in 1995 while there were 3,650 privately owned petrol stations to 1,694 state owned ones.

The agricultural sector employed 26.9% of the workforce in 1996 compared to 9.2% in Spain and 6.7% in France. In 1989 80% of land was in private hands in about 2 million plots averaging 6.3 hectares in size. By 1997 about 130,000 farms had gone to the wall but the average size had barely increased to 7 hectares and 38% of the population still lived in the countryside. About 4 million people still depended upon agriculture but this sector only produced 6.6% of GDP in 1996. The plus side was that greater efficiency drove up the price of land. It encouraged increasing investment, especially from foreign sources, in sectors such as food-processing, brewing and sausage-making in which the Poles had traditional skills, deserved reputations and much cheaper labour forces. Although agriculture is subsidised by KRUS social security funding the problem remains that high unemployment makes it very difficult to decant the rural workforce into urban jobs as in France in the 1950s. At the moment Polish agriculture is divided starkly between the large efficient farms of over 15 hectares mainly in northern and western Poland which make up over half the land and the stagnating small plots of under 5 hectares mainly in southern and eastern Poland. Since 1993 Poland has had a trade deficit with the EU in food products as the Polish producer has developed a taste for higher quality, if more expensive, products; balance has only been maintained by this sector's dynamic performance in eastern markets; this indicates the need for huge investment, in the long-run, in the processing infrastructure as well as in the modernisation of production. The Agricultural Market Agency (ARR) has, since 1990, attempted to achieve price stability and assured farmers' incomes through minimum intervention prices on the CAP model.

Industrial restructuring was also very difficult, as, here as in agriculture, the left-peasant governments had lagged behind with the necessary reforms and only set about some privatisation in 1997. The mid-1990s policy was to combine gradual slimming down with state promoted modernisation and restructuring. Insufficient funds were available, however, most notably at the Ursus tractor factory and in defence industries, to make the latter a real success. On the other hand the manufacturing sector (about four-fifths of the industrial sector) achieved 10% growth rates p.a. in the mid-1990s and made up 30% of domestic output with only a quarter of the workforce. South Korean, Italian and other car producers moved in and also into a number of other high technology sectors. The Warsaw Legia football club adopted the name of its Daewoo sponsor and floated on the stock exchange. Direct foreign investment only picked up after 1994 but by 1996 made up 1.8% of GDP.

The main problem remained how to pension off the large, environmentally damaging and inefficient heavy industry and raw material extraction sector inherited from communism. Labour productivity, for example, was extremely low by world standards in coal mining but strong trade union and political influence ensured that miners received above national average wage increases. The 1993 officially planned decline from 250,000 to 195,000 miners by 2000 fell far below the desired estimated EU entry cut of over a half. Coal output fell from its 1980s level of 190 million tons to 136 million tons in 1995. Total coalmining debts mounted to 10 billion złoties by 1996 but there was insufficient political will to close down 2 of the 7 most heavily subsidised and effectively bankrupt consortia as they employed 60,000 miners. Plans for replacing coal with gas have involved the signing of long-term contracts with Gazprom in Russia. Likewise, although the number of steelworkers had declined from 140,000 in 1990 to 91,000 in 1997, a Canadian Report set a target-figure of 43,000 by 2002 as labour productivity was a quarter of European levels, compared to official hopes of maintaining 75,000. The EU demanded zero steel import duties by 1999 but the Poles kept a 9% rate instead of lowering it to 6% as planned, and demanded additional time up till 2002, notably for the purpose of restructuring the huge Sendzimir (ex-Lenin) works in Nowa Huta and the Katowice Enterprise which between them still employed 50,000 workers and produced 30% of the 35 million tons annual production. Despite the fragmentation of the industry, steel exports still made up 10% of total export sales in 1993. Another important metal, copper, also declined to 11.9 million tons in 1995. Although it was heavily concentrated in the state firm 'Polish Copper' its privatisation was delayed until its shares were sold successfully in Summer 1997. On the other hand Poland's sulphur deposits have underpinned a buoyant chemicals industry. A 1997 World Bank report estimated that Poland still needed to spend between $40–60 billion to repair communism's environmental damage before EU entry.

The private sector in the construction industry held 87% of production by 1995 but it still had not filled the vacuum left by the collapse of the huge housing cooperatives of the communist period. Because of the vast problems of ownership rights and housing finance, credit and maintenance the housing stock was barely being renewed; housing completions fell from about 190,000 in 1985 to 133,000 in 1992 and 58,400 in 1995. A catastrophic shortfall is worsening year by year. Foreign firms tended to join with domestic ones to tender for prestige projects and to consider motorway construction. Private car ownership boomed from 4.8 million in 1989 to 7.2 million in 1994 but was still at about half the Spanish level. Fiat had established cooperation and production links with Poland in the 1970s and still has a major factory in Bielsko Biała. The main FSO works in Warsaw-Żerań was originally taken over by General Motors in the early 1990s but its disappointing investment led it to plan a new factory in Gliwice. Daewoo took over FSO car assembly in 1996. It was forecast that Poland would produce one million motor cars by the year 2000. While the petrol station sector has developed towards largely private ownership the Płock and Gdańsk petrochemical supply monopoly was protected by the 1993–97 governments despite EU protests. Lack of funds has, however, delayed the building of the very necessary 2,500 kilometre long European motorway system across Poland and led to much talk of it being produced entirely on a motorway toll basis. Urban and country roads have deteriorated to dangerous levels because of insufficient upkeep during the last two decades but improvement in this sector will have to await economic take-off. While the state-owned railway has maintained good international lines its domestic network and services declined somewhat. LOT, the state-owned airline, however, upgraded its fleet by buying Western planes in place of its old Soviet ones. Together with the improvement of Warsaw-Okęcie and other airports it has become a prime candidate for early privatisation.

In addition the weak Polish banking, insurance and finance sectors are bound to suffer major bankruptcy and restructuring with the opening up of the economy to Western firms and the break-up of the Social Insurance Trust (ZUS) and similar monopolies (PZU) of the communist period. The banking sector has expanded since 1989 when the National Bank (NBP) had its role of central oversight split from that of commercial banking. The NBP was split in 1993–95 with four of its commercial successors being privatised immediately, another in 1997 and the remaining 4 were scheduled for private control by 1998. The political dangers of privatisation were revealed most starkly by the Silesian Bank affair in early 1994; a huge increase in its initial share price led to allegations of leaks and corruption which brough down finance minister Borowski. The state had majority shareholdings in 24 of the 80 commercial banks, domestic private investment controlled 32 while 24 were foreign controlled. The stock exchange was opened in 1991, very piquantly in the ex-PZPR headquarters on Jerusalem Avenue. It started trading from a very limited base but by 1996 listed 106 companies. The 15 national investment funds included in Belka's mass privatisation scheme of 512 state firms were traded from 1997 onwards. Poland still has a long way to go before the basic aspects of modern capitalism like bank accounts, cash-dispensers, giro payments and cashcards become the norm but the pace of change, especially in the cities, is dramatic. Modern competitive conditions also make it essential to bring domestic Polish tele-communications up to the acceptable standard of its international links. It will cost $15–20 billion to treble Poland's 1995 level of 14.8 telephones per 100 population up to the average European level. The urban average is also 4 times higher than that in the countryside. The pressing nature of the problem, however, did not shift the left-peasant government's reluctance to break up the near monopoly of the state-owned 'Polish Telecommunications' firm.

On the other hand the retailing and service sector has expanded dynamic-ally since 1989. The wild and primitive capitalist retailing of the early 1990s based on street and neighborhood bazaars, car-boots and small kiosks is gradually being replaced by mainly foreign-owned supermarket chains and the whole range of Western brand names such as McDonald's, Coca Cola, Benetton and the like. The big cities are also dominated by foreign-owned hotel chains but native entrepreneurs are predominant in restaurants, estate, accomodation and tourist agencies and the newly sprouting financial, lei-sure, service and other sectors which are largely made up of small private businesses. The latter dominate the firms providing previously unthinkable luxuries like double-glazing, do-it-yourself decorating supplies and all the other joys of the consumer society.

CULTURE AND A MODERN SOCIETY

Poland has now met all the formal tests for democratic consolidation [Taras 1995] although state control of television, aspects of its judicial and administrative processes, political clientelism in the economy, an incoherent party system and residual political and social attitudes of a backward character still arouse concern. Progress towards marketisation has been impressive but is still far from complete. The preceding section has attempted a bird's eye view of the extent to which has Poland has got fit for EU entry and indicated the main remaining problem areas. The rapid progress towards building a democratic market society since 1989 has been so impressive that one is justified in adopting a fairly *Panglossian* view as to the eventual outcome. Until recently academics and external critics were justifiably concerned about the possibility of a cyclical domestic return towards populist-authoritarianism. One can now feel confident in ruling out this possibility as the modernisation process has got a dominating hold of all structures; this aspect of domestic systemic transformation can now be discussed largely in terms of residual blockages and time-scale. Specific issues and normal Europe-wide problems such as the growth of juvenile crime or the spread of firearms replaced systemic questions in the mid-1990s political agenda. What remains controversial is the extent to which mentalities have changed and whether traditional Polish cultural values can survive and maintain a distinct national mould within the democratic capitalist and European framework. The latter question of Poland's external position and the resolution of her traditional security dilemma, the German and Russian threats, through EU and NATO membership will be discussed in the following chapter. Here one should note that the unprecedently favourable external environment has naturally favoured the domestic transformation.

One can only hazard a few concluding observations about the future of *Polskość* and of Polish political culture. Joseph Fiszman pointed out as far back as 1973 that the Marxist–Leninist compromise with traditional Polish values created a mixed version of secular modernisation and a domesticised form of nationalism.[22] With the collapse of communism the issue became not the degree of its internal erosion but the extent to which communist rule had implanted communal and social values and whether the Second Solidarity would turn its civic and self-management rhetoric into reality. The sociologist Włodzimierz Panków forecast the neo-liberal attempt during 1990–93 to dismantle what he called the 'social-democratic infrastructure' inherited from communism but the 'social democratic-populist reaction' of 1993–97 took a much milder form than he had envisaged because of a favourable economic and international environment [Sanford 1992, pp. 195–99]. By 1997 it appeared that the values of egalitarianism and participation had been weakened most by the new market framework while secularism and modern life-styles and de-politicised attitudes had been reinforced. *Poujadist* reactions amongst economically squeezed peasants and industrial workers found expression in Tymiński's 1990 presidential vote and in Lepper's *Samoobrona* but by 1997 were much weaker in the rise of the Pensioners' Party. Authoritarian and racist movements such as Tejkowski's had little electoral success although they provided a violent grass-roots fringe. The integral nationalism of Catholic priests, such as Wałęsa's confessor in his Gdańsk parish, Father Henryk Jankowski, were politically provocative and sullied Poland's international image, but marginal in influence. The same can be said of extremist trade unionists like Zygmunt Wrzodak from Ursus. The populist form of reluctant pro-market and European declarations of the likes of Maciej Jankowski, Solidarity's Mazowsze regional chairman also highlighted the defensive character of much of the AWS formation. The demands for a tough line with the EU, for economic protectionism and for immigration controls voiced by Olszewski's ROP and other nationalist-Catholic groupings may only have appealed directly to barely 5% of the electorate in September 1997 but it was difficult to estimate the extent to which they were supported within the broad and, potentially, fissiparous AWS alliance.

The historical division of attitudes towards the socialist past still provided an important emotional basis for divisions despite crosscutting similarity on policies. A CBOS poll in July 1977 showed that 40% considered that they had lived better under socialism than under the market. Nostalgia for People's Poland was strongest on the left at 46% than on the right at 28%; by party roughly 40% of SLD and PSL supporters throught that the socialist system had brought most people greater benefits than losses while only 20% disagreed and 20% thought that it was about the same. The figures were the other way around for the UW 70% against and 10% in favour, AWS 60% to 10%, ROP 50% against to 10% while the UP predictably, was the most internally divided, 20% both for and against and 50% neutral.[23] The modernisation process and the consolidation of democratic capitalism seemed well on the way to completion but both the post-1989 political camps were internally divided over the desirable pace and final character of the transformation; all that one could forecast safely in 1997 was that, although its general fundamentals were not challenged, it would take a less Anglo-Saxon market and a more social and Polish national cultural form.

1   George Feiwel, *Industrialization and Planning under Polish* Socialism (New York: Praeger, 1971). John Montias, *Central Planning in Poland* (New Haven, CT: Yale UP, 1962).

2   Anders Aslund, *Private Enterprise in Eastern Europe. The non-agricultural private sector in Poland and the GDR, 1945–1983* (London: Macmillan, 1985). Andrzej Korbonski, *Politics of Socialist Agriculture in Poland* (New York: Columbia UP, 1965).

3   Włodzimierz Brus, *The Economics and Politics of Socialism* (London: Routledge, 1973). Jan Drewnowski (ed), *Crisis in the East European Economy. Spread of the Polish Disease* (London: Croom Helm, 1982).

4   Zbigniew Landau & Jerzy Tomaszewski, *The Polish economy in the Twentieth Century* (New York: St Martin's Press, 1984).

5   Johann Arnason, *The Future that Failed* (London: Routledge, 1993).

6   C. Bryant & A. Mokrzycki (eds), *The New Great Transformation?* (London: Routledge, 1994).

7   Andrzej Rychard, *Reforms, Adaptation and Breakthrough.* (Warsaw: IFIS, 1993), pp. 120 ff.

8   Cf. Bogdan Mieczkowski, 'The relationship between changes in consumption and politics in Poland', *Soviet Studies*, vol 30, no 2 (1978), pp. 262–9.

9   George Sanford, *Polish Communism in Crisis* (London: Croom Helm, 1983), pp. 14 ff.

10 Roger Clarke (ed), *Poland. The Economy in the 1980s* (Harlow: Longman, 1989).

11 *The Collapse of State Socialism. The Case of Poland.* (Princeton NJ: Princeton UP, 1991).

12 Jacek Rostowski, 'The decay of socialism and the growth of private enterprise in Poland', *Soviet Studies*, vol 41, no 2 (1989), pp. 194–214.

13 Jadwiga Staniszkis, *The Dynamics of the breakthrough in Eastern Europe. The Polish Experience* (Berkeley: University of California Press, 1991). On the multifaceted character of the reform problem see Andrzej Korbonski, 'The politics of economic reforms in Eastern Europe', *Soviet Studies*, vol 41, no 1 (1989), pp.1–19.

14 Ben Slay, *The Polish Economy. Crisis, Reform and Transformation* (Princeton NJ: Princeton UP, 1994), pp. 86 ff.

15 David Lipton & Jeffrey Sachs, *Creating a market economy: the Polish case. Brookings Papers on Economic Activity* no 1, 1990, pp. 75–147.

16 Cf. George Blazyca & Ryszard Rapacki (eds), *Poland into the 1990s. Economy and Society in Transition* (London: Pinter, 1991). See Stanisław Gomułka and Grzegorz Kołodko in Michael Keren & Gur Offer (eds), *Trials of Transition.* (Boulder, CO: Westview, 1992).

17 Stephen White (ed), *Handbook of Reconstruction in Eastern Europe and the Soviet Union* (Harlow: Longman, 1991), pp. 160–74.

18 Andrew Berg & Olivier Blanchard, 'Stabilization and Transition: Poland 1990–91' in O. Blanchard, K. Froot & J. Sachs (eds), (Chicago: University of Chicago Press, 1994).

19 Kazimierz Poznański, 'Privatisation of the Polish economy', *Soviet Studies*, vol 44, no 4 (1992), pp. 641–64.

20 George Blazyca & Ryszard Rapacki, 'Continuity and change in Polish economic policy: the impact of the 1993 election', *Europe-Asia Studies*, vol 48, no 1 (1996), p. 88.

21 Wherever possible I have drawn statistics in this chapter from *Rocznik Statystyczny 1996* (Warsaw: GUS, 1996). Other useful sources have been the Country Reports and Profiles on Poland produced by the *Economist* Intelligence Unit. The sources for this table are GUS and *Gazeta Wyborcza*, 5 February 1997.

22 Joseph Fiszman, *Revolution and Tradition in People's Poland* (London: Oxford UP, 1973).

23 *Wprost*, 17 August 1997, pp. 21–22.

Chapter 4

POLAND'S PLACE IN THE NEW EUROPE

The consequences of Poland's central location in Europe without defensible frontiers to the east or west have already been discussed in the historical overview in Chapter 1 as have the domestic repercussions in terms of clashing Eastern or Western priorities, and in modern times anti-Russian or anti-German orientations. Adam Bromke married these underlying external factors with domestic dynamics to produce a comprehensive explanation of Poland's modern history in terms of cyclical swings between the dominance of idealist and realist tendencies.[1] His ideas have been criticised but they were accepted as a compelling interpretation until the fundamental transformation of the European framework in the late 1980s.

The collapse of the domestic communist system in Poland was linked integrally to the breakdown of external control by the USSR and to the regaining of the full national sovereignty which had been lost since 1939 and limited since Yalta. The return to traditional balance of power politics might have entailed the resurrection of Poland's national dilemma of surviving between an even more powerful re-united Germany and a weakened, but still dangerous Russia. The resurrection of a belt of weak and small states like Belarus and the Baltic states and of a potentially powerful independent actor like the 52 million strong Ukraine between Poland and Russia could also have been expected to raise as many threats as opportunities. Fortunately for Poland the end of the Cold War and of the ideological-systemic division of Europe did not see the determining Western European part of the continent return to the interwar *realpolitik* law of the international jungle and of unbridled national *raison d'état*.[2] Ethnic conflicts in the former Yugoslavia and USSR have had an intrinsically localised and regional character despite the widening of the Bosnian issue. The new integration framework provided by the European Union (EU) and, after some hesitation, by NATO provided novel answers which transformed Poland's German and Russian problems. Poland's 'Return to Europe' and the emergence of a pan-continental framework has thus provided an exceptionally favourable opportunity for the resolution of her basic security dilemmas. The new Europe and reintegration in the democratic capitalist world also holds out great promise for the resolution of the country's economic backwardness. It has also provided protection against regional threats such as immigration and refugee flows.

Poland has since the 1945 border and population transfers become over 97% ethnically and linguistically homogeneous. She is not threatened by any serious national minority problems although the situation of the Orthodox Ukrainians and (often Protestant) Germans in Poland attracts considerable attention. The Polish majority has been accused of ethnic, and integral-Catholic, nationalism but the spread of more tolerant multicultural and multidenominational attitudes amongst the general population, especially the young and the educated, is an inherent feature of democratisation.

REGAINING SOVEREIGNTY, 1989–91

The Round Table had said little directly about foreign relations. Its participants still accepted the primary restricting character of what were euphemistically called external factors. Gorbachev's 'New Thinking' had, however, led to important revisions in Polish–Soviet relations.[3] The replacement of the Brezhnev Doctrine with the Sinatra principle meant that Soviet intervention was increasingly unlikely. Previously unmentionable 'blank spots' such as the Hitler-Stalin Pact of 1939 were acknowledged while the authorities even squared up cautiously to the Katyń issue. But this, as with so much of last-ditch reform communism in Poland, remained largely an elite and intellectual affair without much popular resonance. The late 1980s East–West *detente* has been described as 'opening up a conjunction without precedent for Poland since 1945, and perhaps even in the whole of her modern history'.[4] The primary reason that the Mazowiecki government was able to redefine Poland's foreign, as well as domestic and economic, policy was largely because of the rapid collapse of the remainder of the East European communist bloc in late 1989. Mazowiecki, in his initial Sejm *exposé,* said that his government would respect Poland's existing international obligations but he called for the building of a new Europe which would 'overcome the world's postwar divisions'.[5] The new, non-communist foreign minister, Krzysztof Skubiszewski (born 1926), remained in his post through the four governments of Mazowiecki, Bielecki, Olszewski and Suchocka. He was a much respected professor of international law at Poznań university who had advised Cardinal Glemp on his Social Council. His main initial tasks in the transitional period until 1991 were threefold: firstly, to ensure that Poland's interests would not be harmed by the reunification of Germany; secondly, to disentangle Poland from Soviet control and to balance between Russia and the other republics in the process leading up to the dissolution of the USSR in December 1991; thirdly, to re-establish full sovereignty in the international arena and to begin the process of gradually realigning Poland with Western Europe.

Fears of German revisionism were truly genuine and widespread in post-war Poland. They were fanned instrumentally by the authorities in order to drum up support for communism and the Soviet alliance which guaranteed Poland's possession of the Recovered Territories; this does not undermine the strength of national concern on this issue even after the the 1970 treaty. The division of Germany was thus always welcome to many Poles. Its unification in 1990 raised strong fears; these were fanned by unwise statements by Chancellor Kohl and by spokesmen of German expellee organisations. Skubiszewski was, therefore, primarily concerned to protect Poland's interests at the 'two plus four' talks between the two German states and the four wartime allied powers. Poland did not oppose German unification but wanted the new 79 million strong state and economic giant to be tied down to European security structures. Kohl backed down from his initial attempts to gain concessions for the German minority in Poland and to force Warsaw to waive war-reparation rights. In the end the Bundestag and President von Weizsacker confirmed Poland's frontiers before Germany was unified on 2 October. The inviolability of the Polish–German border was guaranteed formally and without qualification in the Treaty of 14 November 1990.[6]

Wałęsa and his camp accused Skubiszewski in the run-up to the 1990 presidential election of being mesmerised by the German question and consequently, too slow and cautious in disentangling Poland from the decaying Soviet framework. The most emotional issue was that of the withdrawal of the Soviet garrison of about 40,000 which had been stationed in the Legnica region under Gomułka's agreement of December 1956. Jaruzelski and Mazowiecki wanted Poland's security to be guaranteed against Germany in the first instance. The Polish demand for full withdrawal and compensation for damage was, therefore, delayed until September 1990. Negotiations were to drag on for 18 months and involved provocative statements by General Victor Dubinin, the Soviet garrison comander in Poland. They were only resolved in principle after Yeltsin came to power and completed when Wałęsa visited Moscow in May 1992. The real problem was the use of Poland for transit for the 20 Russian divisions in the ex-East Germany who had to leave by 1994. Wałęsa and Olszewski made continual demagogic use of the issue during 1991–92 linking it with criticism of Skubiszewski's cautious 'dual track' policy towards the USSR until its final break-up in December 1991. Comecon was wound up officially in June 1991 and the Warsaw Pact in July confirming Skubiszewski's wisdom in avoiding Poland's premature embroilment in the east. The 1991 election and the end of the contractual Sejm thus also marked the shift to a fully independent foreign policy.

The priority now became overwhelmingly *westpolitik* and to a subsidiary extent, central European regional concerns.

Skubiszewski defined the main principles of Polish foreign policy as follows in the Sejm on 21 January 1993.[7] Polish *raison d'état* was superior to all domestic divisions and he quoted Piłsudski and Dmowski on the need for agreed guiding ideas. His were the protection of national interests from externally imposed decisions but involved balanced co-operation with both stronger and weaker partners. He identified the country's strategic priorities since 1989 as growing alignment with West European and Atlanticist structures, the joint creation of a pan-European security system, the development of cordial relations with neighbours and the strengthening of regional links. 'The supreme interests of the state and nation' dictated that Poland should build on the EU association agreement and work for full entry. Only this would assure the consolidation of democracy and market reform, stimulate agricultural and financial transformation and protect the country from the dangers of instability to the east. Skubiszewski developed the latter theme in his Sejm report of 29 April 1993, stressing the positive aspects of the North Atlantic Co-operation Council (NACC) in assisting military and security collaboration in the region. 'The disintegration of the USSR and the emergence of a number of independent states aiming at a democratic political and economic transformation has changed Poland's geopolitical situation to our advantage and created a peculiar historic opportunity.' What was striking, however, was the extent to which Skubiszewski predicated the establishment of good neighbourly relations with them on their becoming 'an integral part of the European system in its various dimensions'.[8] That the Polish commitment to EU and NATO membership should be viewed as encouraging democratisation and economic reform in the post-Soviet republics and as a deterrent against a relapse into authoritarianism and imperialism in Russia were constantly reiterated Polish themes.[9]

Poland's defence and security options chrystallised in two MON documents in November 1992. These identified no immediate threat but committed Poland's long term security to NATO membership and multilateral collaboration. The above mentioned political themes were reflected in an academic debate in the early 1990s redefining the principles, style and geo-strategic interests of Polish foreign policy.[10] This involved a complete shift from the chimera of the *realpolitik* pursuit of the national self-interest of the Polish state to a wider understanding of how this interest could only be achieved within the new multilateral and collaborative Euro-Atlantic framework.[11]

Poland has always been an active member of international organisations (UN, WHO, IBRD, GATT in 1967, IMF in 1986, etc). After 1989 Poland joined the European Bank for Reconstruction and Development (EBRD, 1990), the Council of Europe (CE, 1991) and the Organisation for Economic Co-operation and Development (OECD) in 1996.

Although communism collapsed in Poland in 1989 the post-communist state of her neighbours only emerged with the dissolution of the USSR in 1991 and the Czech–Slovak split as of January 1993. What was unprecedented was that although Poland did not shift her frontiers all 7 of her current neighbours changed in one respect or other. The Ukraine (52 million, sharing a 529 kilometre frontier with Poland), Belarus (10.2 million, 416 kilometres) and Lithuania (3.75 million, 103 kilometres) were completely new independent states while the Czech Republic (10.3 million, 790 kilometres) and Slovakia (5.27 million, 539 kilometres) emerged out of Czechoslovakia. The German Democratic Republic (18 million) vanished completely and was replaced by a united and extended Federal Republic of Germany (79 million, 467 kilometres). Poland no longer shared a frontier with the new Russian Federation except with the now isolated Kaliningrad province (Królewiec in Polish, 210 kilometres). Poland also had 524 kilometres of coastline on the Baltic sea. Some analysts explained Poland's geo-political position in the 1990s in terms of a fundamental return to its Piast rather than Jagiellonian form and orientation. Historians like Jerzy Krasucki argued that, now, as in the Piast period, Poland had to come to terms with German domination. Polish–German interests could be squared in developing the post-Russian space; his very Polish-cultural, as against Anglo-Saxon market, view was that 'Western civilisation is not identical with capitalism'.[12]

Poland's place in Europe also changed fundamentally; from being surrounded by Warsaw Pact and Comecon partners and definitely in Eastern Europe she now found herself, in the early 1990s, in an undefined no man's land between the EU and the Commonwealth of Independent States (CIS). With her 38.6 million, very homogeneous and well educated population her central position as a medium-sized regional power now offered more potential benefits than dangers as in the past. Her political elites in 1991 were fairly united that Poland's priority was to embed herself in the Western EU and NATO structures and, hopefully, to become the third leg of a French-German–Polish axis. Only then could she carry out an effective Eastern policy from this Western base. This ruled out Moczulski's and the KPN's risky great power option of Poland as the historically best-fitted organiser of the eastern borderlands setting up an effective barrier against the Russian danger. On the other hand there were no such problems with the minor and wholly collaborative version of regional collaboration with southern neighbours.

One might also mention that democratic Poland inherited an enormous burden of international indebtedness from the communist period. This totalled about $50 billion in late 1992 but satisfactory debt rescheduling agreements and write-offs were achieved by 1994. Debt-servicing was further reduced by the strong growth of exports. By 1995 only 10% of export-earnings were required to service debt-repayment compared to 70% in 1991. Poland thus entered and benefited from, the international money markets. Debt repayments will, however, pick up in the early years of the next century and will have to be repaid to the Paris Club by 2014 and the London Club by 2024.

While there was great sympathy especially in the successor-communist and peasant camps for the CSCE (subsequently OCSE), in which Poland had played a determined role from 1975 onwards, and pan-European initiatives the main thrust from 1991 onwards was decidedly towards embedding Poland in the European Union (EU) and bodies such as the Western European Union (WEU), NACC and the Partnership for Peace which opened up the way to NATO entry. These two central themes will now be examined; this will be followed by discussion of Poland's relations with her neighbours and her regional policy.

EUROPEAN UNION

Polish academics considered that East–West bipolarism was replaced by a loose form of American dominated unipolarism after 1989. Apart from the fate of the new Russian and successor-Soviet republics the continental issue which concerned them most of all was how the post-Maastricht balance between deepening and widening would affect Polish relations with the EU. Slogans such as Gorbachev's 'Common European Home' or Mitterrand's 'common organisation for peace and security' were quickly seen to be illusory. The Poles, therefore, concentrated on post-totalitarian transformation as the key to remedying the asymetric character of relations between Western and Eastern Europe.[13]

The EEC (EC, as it was then) established official relations with Comecon in June 1988 and signed a trade and economic agreement on 19 September 1989 which accorded Poland most favoured nation trade relations.[14] The EC, despite its preoccupation with implementing the Single European Act and negotiating Maastricht, began talks with Poland which culminated in the agreement of 17 December 1991 on associate membership.[15] This Europe Agreement, whose passing in the Sejm by 238 votes to 78 with 20 abstentions in July 1992 reflected the growth of some opposition to its costs, laid down a

10 year period of tariff reduction. These were to begin in early 1994, with asymetric short-term benefits in Poland's favour initially but with subsequent opening up of the Polish economy to more advanced industrial and manufacturing competitors; but it excluded agriculture and did not contain a comitment to full membership. The latter came subsequently and was predicated on the consolidation of democracy and market capitalism in Poland as well as the redefinition of her legal norms and regulations to meet European standards.

By 1993 Poland had established herself as a member of a leading group, of four countries, which best met the criteria for EU membership. She was, however, considered a touch behind Hungary, Slovenia and the Czech Republic in terms of infrastructure and economic development as well as culturally more resistant to market liberalism.[16] That Poland was in the first rank of potential entrants was crucial as the EU Copenhagen summit of June 1993 decided to move on from the previous policy of PHARE assistance and association to identifying problems of full membership with candidates with an eye to accelerating their resolution. Thus encouraged, and in the light of EFTA–EU amalgamation and the forthcoming enlargement taking in Finland, Sweden and Austria, Poland lodged its full membership application in April 1994. Although the Sejm supported the application unanimously this was more in general value terms of rejoining Western civilisation rather than for specific political or economic reasons.

The PSL wing of the Pawlak government doubted whether Brussels would either be willing to extend full CAP benefits or open EU markets to Polish agricultural products. The cost of CAP subsidies for Poland at the 1997 level was estimated by the World Bank at $5.2 billion annually. In general Polish public opinion had moved on from its initial uncritical Euro-enthusiasm but according to CBOS polls overwhelming majorities of between 70–88% supported the principle of EU membership from 1992–97. This masked a greater and spreading awareness of the economic gap between it and even the poorest EU Mediterranean members, the enormous costs and long time-scale, well past 2000, of the transition as well as the moving-target character of EU membership. Average per capita GDP in Poland was $2,484 in 1994, compared to $5,600 for Portugal, $6,700 for Greece, $10,600 for Ireland, $12.500 for Spain and at the other end $24,400 for Belgium and an EU average of $20,000. Despite all this the Poles took the long-view and attempted to maintain a common Višegrad front in the Brussels negotiations. The Poles have few direct conflicts with the Czechs and Hungarians but they were soon forced to realise the mutually competitive character of their EU application.[17]

The level of public knowledge was difficult to judge as over half of the population in September 1996 thought that EU entry would not limit Poland's sovereignty while 34% thought that it would and 66% had no objection to the ECU replacing the *złoty*. Jacek Saryusz-Wolski, the government commissioner for European Integration considered in Summer 1996 that four fifths of the EU entry problem depended upon the success of Poland's domestic tranformation effort. But building a market economy did not mean that Poland should not protect her interests, specially infant industries or sectors threatened by uncurbed free trade. For example, Poland's continuing protection of her strategic petrochemicals sector and resistance to EU pressure for rapid privatisation of the energy sector led to public criticism by the EU Commissioner for the Eastern Enlargement, Hans van den Broek. Foreign minister Rosati in return argued that despite short-term shortages premature opening up of the petrol and oil sector to foreign competition would lead to the bankruptcy of potentially viable units like the Płock petrochemicals firm. Van den Broek had also expressed Brussels' displeasure at the signing of an agreement which allowed Daewoo, the South Korean motor car manufacturer, to assemble 110,000 cars, worth $1.4 billion, tariff-free at the old FSO factory.[18] Warsaw backed down in face of stiff warnings that such tariff concessions would complicate its subsequent EU entry negotiations. Another typically European spat occurred in April 1997 when the Poles, under strong EU Commission (and Spanish) pressure, had to abandon their attempt to levy 22% VAT on citrus imports.

Although hardly anybody in the Polish political and academic elite saw any alternative to EU entry the potential timetable of the EU Governmental Conference agreeing to Eastern Enlargement in 1997, opening negotiations with potential new members by April 1998, completing the agreements in 2000 and ratifying them leading to full membership by the year 2002, struck many as unduly optimistic. The problem was the size of the economic and infrastructural gap between Poland and the EU average which it was calculated would need a billion dollars to make up by 2000. Poland's 1996 inflation rate of 19% and interest rate of 22% were well above the Maastricht convergence criteria but the budget and public debt levels were quite acceptable. Austerity and a fall in real incomes were, however, inevitable prices of the necessary restructuring—the only question being how much and for how long.

The most contentious problems of agricultural and industrial restructuring have already been discussed in Chapter 3. Minister of agriculture Jagieliński's dictum that about 30% of Poland's farms could compete at EU levels, that another 40% could be brought up to this level and that 30% were bound to go to the wall driving a minimum 800,000 individuals out of agriculture gained wide currency. Rosati confirmed that the question of the access of Polish agricultural products to EU markets would be one of the most difficult issues in the entry negotiations. It was also unclear whether CAP would be reformed by 2000 while Polish hopes of negotiating high quotas receded as their EU trade deficits in foodstuffs increased during 1996. The vast shrinkage of employment required in coal mining and steel production and the threats to the shipbuilding, copper and other industrial sectors have already been indicated.

Unemployment had momentarily dipped to 14% but was likely to increase to Spanish levels of 20–25% at the trough of the entry period. The great hope was that the commercial, retailing and services sector of 13.7% (1993) would double in size reaching average European levels within the decade. Everybody repeated that there was no alternative to EU entry but Polish society had been conditioned to oppose economic reality and price-increases on ideological grounds since 1970. This had been a major factor in provoking the crises which eventually brought down communism. Despite the political and social demobilisation since 1989 and the possibility of foreign work outlets one can only wonder whether Poland will be willing to take all this harsh economic medicine quietly. On the other hand the Spanish comparison of similar populations, Catholic cultures and great nation traditions was also on everybody's lips as a talisman for remedying Poland's two decade's long stagnation; following Franco's death in 1974, rapid economic take-off and liberalisation had increased Spain's GDP to about 6 times that of Poland's and modernised her society and place in Europe.

Olechowski in 1997 saw EU membership as consolidating Poland's international position, opening up Western markets to her goods and giving her the chance of influencing decisions which would affect her anyway. Poland should already begin to think of affecting the EU's policy towards greater enlargement and the development of the remaining East European markets. But an OBOP poll in April 1997 showed that what Poles feared most about EU entry was the following; 41% excessive buying up of the economy by foreign capital, 31% the collapse of agriculture, 23% increased unemployment, 18% increased emigration, 14% industrial decline, 11% decline in standard of living and 9% that border provinces would be lost to neighbours.

A powerful coalition of anti-European opinion developed most strongly within ROP, ZChN, PSL and right wing and Catholic strands within Solidarity. This fuelled the view that the only remaining important division in Polish foreign policy attitudes was between nationalists and pro-Europeans. Nationalist forces joined with the fear of the Roman Catholic church that a liberal and materialist Poland with open frontiers and weak sovereignty would lose her cultural distinctiveness, and her religious beliefs. The decline of industry and agriculture plus large-scale labour emigration in the early phases of EU entry would further weaken the church's membership base and social and cultural implantation. Despite such fears a liberal wing of the church hierarchy, led by Bishop Józef Życiński of Tarnów, re-iterated Pope John Paul's message during his Summer 1997 visit that the answer to the post-1989 flood of pornography and narcotics was not to close Poland's frontiers but to work for a more spiritual Europe. Glemp, balanced by patronising a European Studies Centre in the Warsaw Theological Academy, supported by Olechowski and the pro-European conservative right, and funded by the Soros, Adenauer and Batory foundations.

About one third of Poland's trade in the communist period had been with the USSR and another third with other communist states. By 1995 the EU had become Poland's largest trade partner while Poland was the EU's seventh largest; 70% of Polish exports went to, while 65% of her imports came from, the EU. The problem was that EU exports to Poland (machinery and electrical goods 27% of total) trebled between 1989 and 1995 while Polish exports to the EU (base metals 17%) only doubled leaving a deficit of 2.8 billion ECU. Poland's remaining trade exchanges were with Central Europe (17% exports/15% imports) and Russia (6% exports/7% imports).

Poland had prepared its European case administratively as follows; the reform of the governmental machine in October 1996 established a ministerial committee for European integration, chaired by the prime minister, to co-ordinate and oversee policies in this field. Its office also checked draft Polish legislation to ensure its compatibility with EU norms. A National Integration Strategy, published in early 1997, prepared for EU accession by identifying the required policies and the 5 sectors where Poland needed special transitional arrangements. Encouraged by the 1995 EU Commission White Paper on the measures to be taken by prospective candidates in order to prepare for the Internal Market all Polish ministries set up EU integration units. Another 33 working groups, about 500 individuals, implemented the preparatory Stage I measures. Poland also participated in the Structured Dialogue process as well as in a wide range of community programmes. PHARE, for example committed another 203 million ECU in 1996 to restructuring agriculture, banking and financial, social and environmental services. The aim of all this activity was to align Poland's institutions, policies and legal framework with EU practice thus building up what is termed the *acquis communitaire*.

The EU Amsterdam summit in June 1997, concluding a year-long Intergovernmental Conference, was criticised for its failure to resolve its institutional problems, especially the reweighting of Council votes. It took the crucial decision, however, to begin entry negotiations with 5 of the 10 East European applicants (Poland, Czech Republic, Hungary, Slovenia and Estonia). The EU Commission published its opinion on the state of these 10 applications as part of its Agenda 2000 in mid-July. At the same time it unveiled proposals for overhauling CAP and regional policy and promised funds of $59 billion for applicants who entered the EU by 2006.

As far as Poland was concerned the commission reported its long and detailed 122 page 'Opinion' on its application on 15 July 1997.[19] Following the 1993 Copenhagen criteria for membership the commission gave Poland's political system and institutions a clean bill of health in assuring democracy, the rule of law, human rights and minority protection. Improvements were called for in the judicial system, especially to root out corruption and to assure property restitution. The freedom of the press and political control of state-run TV also aroused concern. The commission confirmed that Poland was 'a functioning market economy' which had stabilised the economy and liberalised prices and trade successfully. The banking and financial sectors needed further development while pensions and social security required a basic overhaul. It was confident that Poland could cope with the EU's competitive and market pressures as long as it continued restructuring agriculture and its remaining state-owned industrial enterprises. Inflows of foreign investment were promising and compensated for the ups and downs in trade so the prime need, according to Brussels, was to keep the economy as open as possible. The commission identified numerous shortfalls in Poland's capacity to take on membership obligations relating to the single market (public procurement, data protection, competition and liberalisation of capital movements) but praised the progress achieved on company law, taxation, accounting, financial services and intellectual property. Much of the Europe Agreement had been implemented satisfactorily but 'too many trade-related problems have arisen'. Legislative adaptation was proceeding satisfactorily except in the field of technical rules and standards. The sectors needing the greatest effort to bring them up to European standards to meet the *acquis* were fisheries, telecommunications, consumer protection, transport and the environment. Industry, energy, employment and social affairs and regional policy and cohesion met with surprisingly sanguine reports while agriculture was generally glossed over in politically pudic terms. So was the issue of Poland's capacity to participate eventually in the third stage of economic and monetary union. Drugs, border management and crossborder crime set Poland considerable problems but the removal of border controls with EU members (Germany and Czech Republic) was within her medium term capacity. The absence of territorial disputes with neighbours meant that Poland should have no problems with the Union's common foreign and security policy. The commission thus recommended the opening of negotiations for Poland's accession to the EU. It promised to submit another report by end 1998 on the progress which Poland had achieved in tackling the problems and shortfalls identified in the 'Opinion'.

NATO AND SECURITY ISSUES

NATO had originally been designed as a military pact to defend Western Europe against the threat of Soviet and Warsaw Pact aggression. With Gorbachev's disarmament and confidence-building agreements, the ending of the division of Europe through the collapse of communism and the break-up of the USSR its traditional function shifted in a more political direction. Polish policy up to 1991 was to disentangle herself from remaining Warsaw Pact involvements and to negotiate the withdrawal of the Soviet garrison. Her governments during 1991–93 were inclined to view NATO membership as providing guarantees against any renewal of the Russian threat and, therefore, as extending the Atlanticist security zone as far as the Bug.

The Americans and their Western European allies, however, took a long-term view. They were primarily concerned to continue the great power military and nuclear disarmament started by Gorbachev and Reagan at the Reykjavik summit in 1987. They, therefore, followed through with START I in July 1991, START II in January 1993 and renegotiated the 1990 Conventional Forces Agreement in 1997. As well as laying down cuts in the size of military forces and their equipment and a diminution in nuclear arsenals these agreements made it possible for Belarus, Kazahkstan and the Ukraine to hand over the nuclear missiles stationed on their territory to Russia. By 1997 all short and medium range nuclear weapons had been removed from Europe while NATO had reduced its nuclear warhead capacity by 80% compared to 1990. All this was accompanied by troop-surveillance, monitoring and movement measures on the confidence-building front which had by 1997 reduced the threat of general, as against local, military conflict in Europe close to nil.

The second main NATO and American aim, running alongside the former, was to encourage democratic and market development in Russia after Yeltsin took over in 1991. Much was done to prevent Russia from feeling isolated and threatened by NATO moves into what had previously been her post-Yalta sphere of influence or empire. The Clinton administration, working closely with Kohl's Germany, banked on the Russian card to the extent of beginning START III talks even before the ratification of its predecessor.

They conceded that NATO nuclear weapons and troop formations would not be stationed on the territory of new entrants. Although hardline Russian reactions to proposed NATO enlargement sent tremors through Warsaw, Prague and Budapest in 1996–97 Moscow and Washington were really engaged in a bargaining process which culminated in the Paris Founding Act for NATO–Russian Consultation of 27 May 1997. Russia lifted her veto on NATO enlargement and indicated that she would sign bilateral security agreements with her neighbours, notably the Ukraine. The establishment of a new NATO–Russia Council with a permanent secretariat gave the latter what was termed a voice, but not a veto, in Western security affairs. Chirac described the agreement as finally erasing all signs of the Cold War and the Yalta division of Europe. Russia was, thus, associated with a NATO, which assumed a pan-European and political character; it nevertheless still retained an important military-psychological aspect for the potential Polish, Czech and Hungarian partners agreed at the Madrid summit.

NATO membership was, therefore, much delayed and came in somewhat looser form than originally desired by Poland. She worked with the alliance initially through the North Atlantic Co-operation Council (NACC) established in December 1991. This marked Poland's symbolic break with the Warsaw Pact and the shift towards links, consultation and the exchange of information with NATO. The multilateral Partnership for Peace (PfP), launched in January 1994, was seen as giving priority to the wider American aim of consolidating the post-communist region (27 OCSCE members, including Russia, joined by late 1995) rather than as catering for specific Polish national security needs. Poland, nevertheless, had joined by 2 February and was the first to conclude an individual Partnership Programme with NATO in July 1994 within the PfP. She established liason offices at NATO and SHAPE and agreed guidelines for modernising Poland's air defence and for making it and other Control and Command systems compatible with Western ones. Foreign minister Olechowski viewed participation in NATO's Planning and Review Process, which this permitted, as an important channel for asserting the country's interest in NATO membership and in preparing for it. Steps towards interoperability were developed by Poland's enthusiastic, if small-scale, participation in the IFOR (and later SFOR) peacekeeping forces in the former Yugoslavia. One might mention here that Polish public opinion was pro-Croatian and anti-Serb and sympathised strongly with Bosnia as a victim of aggression. The government also saw the economic benefits of participating in its reconstruction.[20] Poland thus laid the groundwork for security guarantees and established numerous institutional links, even before full NATO membership.

By 1997, with Yeltsin's re-election as president, the possibility of an authoritarian relapse in Russia leading to the reassertion of its imperial control, or even some sort of sphere of influence in Central and Eastern Europe had become marginal, for the moment. So had the likelihood that the northern tier of Central Europe at least, would be rent by the resurgence of national and great power rivalries. The ending of the security vacuum in Central Europe and the anchoring of Poland in Atlanticist economic and security structures thus led Clinton in October 1996 to announce that the time was right for NATO enlargement but to limit it to 3 members. Poland's access to NATO, together with that of Hungary and the Czech Republic, was finally agreed at Madrid on 8 July 1997 as was a timetable envisaging negotiations and ratification by members during 1998 and full membership in 1999.

Poland's military forces had been equipped almost entirely from Warsaw Pact sources and according to its standards. Her war industry was quite small and post-communist conversion to non-military production raised no major problems;[21] by 1993 it had about 80 plants, of which only 30 were significant, making up one per cent of all industrial production compared to 3% in 1989. Meeting NATO standards meant an expensive updating of everything from aircraft and tanks to basic ammunition. It stimulated a discussion about the balance between domestic production and expensive imports from Western or alternative sources such as Israel or Brazil. The prime cases in 1996–97 were the already discussed replacement of MiG fighters and of a new avionics system for the Huzar helicopter. The Polish view was that the cost of re-equipping and restructuring their army to meet NATO requirements could be spread out over a decade. Onyszkiewicz, for example, claimed that the new air-defence and communications system, costing $1,500 million, could be phased in over 15 years. MON estimated the cost of modernising the armed forces at $8 billion but calculated that this could be met out of economic growth and by numerical slimming down and base-closures.

BILATERAL RELATIONS

Germany

With democracy becoming entrenched in Poland as well as in united Germany, with frontiers becoming obsolete and with both committed to the building of the new Europe it was argued that German–Polish relations could now be redefined. The shift was a fundamental historical one from conflict to collaboration. The sentiment favouring the burying of historical resentments and animosities was strongest in Poland amongst the young and in Solidarity circles. This vista opened up with the declaration of 14 November

1989 which traced out new paths of political, economic, social and cultural collaboration. That Germany became Poland's most important bilateral partner in the transitional 1990s after centuries of conflict, when they regarded each other as *erstfiende* (eternal enemies), is only an apparent paradox. Statesman on both sides repeated the cliché that Germany's road to the East lay through Poland while Poland's road to Europe and the West lay through Germany but that their relationship was now wholly co-operative. Germany became Poland's essential interlocutor in the council chambers of the EU, NATO and the West. German investment was also crucial to the successful modernisation of the Polish economy. What had historically been a primary French alliance for the Poles thus also became somewhat subsidiary in the new Weimar Triangle (France-Germany-Poland).

Prussia had attempted to Germanise the Poles in its partition area in Pomerania, Poznania and Silesia before the First World War. The Germany minority of about 80,000 in interwar Poland became the archetype *Fifth Column* when Hitler's demands for the cession of Danzig (Gdańsk) and the extra-territorial road to East Prussia across the Polish Corridor provoked the outbreak of the Second World War. The Germans became the privileged *Volksdeutche* who participated in Nazi rule and in its crimes. Hardly surprisingly, the bulk fled before the approach of the Red Army in 1944–45. The remaining Germans understandably adopted a low profile under communist rule. They were denied the normal cultural and linguistic minority rights except departure to the Federal Republic after the 1970 treaty. Estimates of the size of the post-1989 German minority are highly contested as German governments have claimed all one million individuals of pre-1914 German descent irrespective of their degree of Polonisation. A figure of 350,000, where the German element of the dual identity is not weaker than the Polish, is the most likely; official Polish sources concede generously that it might range up to 500,000. This is even more difficult to estimate because of the presence of intermediate or authochtonous groups, notably the Cassubians, Mazurians and Silesians who numbered 1.1 million in the 1950 census. Both categories declined significantly with the emigration of 988,000 individuals to the Federal Republic between 1950–1988.

No less than 32 German cultural, social and charitable groups were organised by 1992. Their actual membership indicates the main concentrations in Opole (200,000), Katowice (60,000) and Częstochowa (30,000) provinces. They demanded dual language signposting of road and other signs and the use of German in official proceedings in areas where Germans were a majority. Many also held dual Polish–German nationality according to the laws of the Federal Republic as they or their parents had been born within 1937

Reich frontiers. This raised problems as dual nationality is forbidden by Polish law. German Minority parties elected 7 deputies to the Sejm and a Senator in 1991, 4 Sejm deputies in 1993 and another 2 in 1997. They also gained considerable representation in the local elections of 1990 and 1994, especially in the Opole and Racibórz regions.

The Polish complaint about the lack of recognition accorded to the Polish minority in Germany, which as a result of labour emigration during the 1980s totalled about a million, was partly regulated by the good neighbourliness and collaboration treaty of 17 June 1991. The problem was that German law does not have the concept of national minorities compared to the full recognition of the rights of the German minority in Poland. Polish sensitivities were also bruised by demands for *Wehrmacht* service to be pensionable and for military service in the Bundeswher to be recognised by the Polish authorities. Polish public opinion still harbours residual fears of the German *Drang nach ocsten,* although direct military threats seem non-existent under present circumstances. Polls regularly show Germany to be one of the countries least trusted by the Poles but the fear at the moment is one of gradual encroachment and that Germany would abuse its economic power to extort political concessions; hence the fear in some circles about Euroregions and the purchase of land or property by Germans. The Germans attempted to soothe Polish sensitivities from Willy Brandt onwards with symbolic gestures of national reconciliation asking forgiveness for German war-crimes during the Second World War notably at commemorations of the Warsaw ghetto and 1944 uprisings. School textbooks have also been rewritten by both sides since the 1970 treaty. Border crossing facilities have been increased and improved and crossborder cultural links, economic collaboration, joint projects and shopping expeditions have boomed since 1989.[22] On the other hand it has proved difficult to animate the proposed Neisse Euroregion in the environmentally damaged triangle where Germany, Poland and the Czech Republic meet.

Russia and Kaliningrad

Historical experience has left the Poles with ambivalent attitudes towards Russia made up of a mixture of cultural superiority, a liking for Russians as individuals and for their culture as well as fear of Russian aggression. Unhappy memories of Russian rule during the partition and Soviet periods and of Stalin's stab in the back in September 1939 provide the basis for widespread national hostility. These were fanned by Soviet intervention in Lithuania in 1990 and the possibility of an authoritarian-imperialist relapse associated with Zhirinovsky's rise after 1993. On the other hand the Poles do not now share a common border with Russia except in Kaliningrad. They benefit from a certain buffer in the independent Lithuanian, Ukrainian and Belarus states, the first two of whom are resolutely anti-Russian. Only the extremely old now have any nostalgia for the pre-September 1939 eastern border expressed in the words of a famous song pining for the return of Lwów.

The rejection of communism was so closely linked to the expulsion of the Soviet Russian hegemon that Polish national attitudes and politics were bound to be long affected. As we have seen the agreement establishing a timetable for the withdrawal of Russian troops in Poland was only completed in Moscow in May 1992 and the last operational units only left in September 1993. Polish claims for compensation for the environmental damage which they had caused were not satisfied while some of the bases themselves retained a residual Russian presence in the form of joint stock enterprises. The issue divided the Wałęsa and Mazowiecki wings of Solidarity while the successsor-communist forces (SdRP and PSL) were attacked continually by the national-independence camp (KPN and Christian-National) for residual financial links and unpatriotic machinations with Moscow. Such emotions and fears provided the emotional underpinning for the Oleksy affair. Even the commercial and foreign trade treaty signed in Warsaw in August 1993 proved difficult to judge purely on its objective merits.

Poland welcomed the beginnings of some sort of democracy under Yeltsin, despite his Chechnya misadventure, and his tortuous rapprochment with NATO leading to the 1997 Paris agreement. Olszewski and Wałęsa reverted to some traditional historical attitudes about their country's barrier role in Eastern Europe after 1991 and attempted to isolate Russia. By 1993 though, the emphasis had clearly shifted to another historical plank, that of their role as a bridge to the East especially in the Europeanisation of Russia. Warsaw's fears during 1991–97 were that Russia would veto Poland's integration in NATO thus causing a security vacuum in Central Europe. Russian policy, in what it considered its 'Near-Abroad', and its reassertion in what had been its Inner-Empire, were the other main area of concern. Despite the general failure of the CIS the main lines of Poland's Eastern policy after 1989, involving the replacement of the Soviet Russian Warsaw Pact security system and Poland's shift into the Euro-Atlantic NATO framework provided the dominant issue for Polish–Russian relations until 1997. The sensitive issues on the minor level of their bilateral relations were, however, also resolved by that date. Russian troops left Poland, the documents clarifying the 1939 Ribbentrop-Molotov Pact as laying the basis for the Fourth Partition of Poland as well as Stalin's responsibility for Katyń were made public. Liberals in both countries called for the truth to be revealed about Stalin's other repressions involving the deportations of Poles from the Eastern Territories in 1940.

Successive censuses showed a decline in the size of the Polish minority in Russia from 118,400 in 1959 to 94,600 in 1989 but these figures do not take a high degree of intermarriage and assimilation into account which affects over a million people. It is estimated that barely 15% consider Polish to be their mother tongue so it is fair to surmise that the majority have been Russified.

Poland does not play an important role in Russian policy following far behind the USA and China in global political terms and Germany and Japan in economic ones. The main issues at stake during Yeltsin's August 1993 visit to Warsaw involved Russian agreement to Polish NATO membership (Yeltsin's 'understanding' for the Polish position was backtracked subsequently) and the breakdown in Polish–Russian trade. The September 1991 agreement to replace the transferable rouble and Soviet barter type exchanges with hard currency led to a fall of 45% in Polish exports and about a third in imports. About 80% of Polish imports were in essential petrol and gas supplies so Poland was left with a considerable bilateral trade deficit. The building of the Friendship gas-pipeline through Poland and on to Germany was envisaged as lessening these costs in future. It would enable Poland's gas imports to rise from 6 billion square metres to 14 billion square metres by 2010 while Poland would benefit directly from 15% of its construction. The transitional costs of the economic transformation were considered worthwhile on both sides. About 900 joint-ventures were already functioning in Russia with 100% Polish capital participation. It was hoped that such professional economic activity would soon replace the rock-bottom merchant-tourist trading flourishing in Warsaw's Tenth Anniversary football stadium and in the neighbourhood bazaars of all Polish cities in the early 1990s. Olechowski stressed the importance of rebuilding Russo–Polish trade relations at his February 1994 Kraków meeting with foreign minister Kozyrev. But the rhetoric of his Transformation for Peace framework proved somewhat premature.

One of the most popular 1989 slogans, that of a Europe without frontiers, eventually enabled Poles to travel to the West without visas. In late 1996 visas were abolished for crossings into Poland by Russians but the situation was complicated on the eastern frontier as the crossing points could not cope with the flood of 21 million crossings in 1995 and the regular merchant-tourism across the frontier. In addition it was estimated that up to two and a half million Russians and other ex-Soviet people have settled permanently in Poland, many working illegally and cheaply. Large numbers are also involved in criminal gangs or in parallel activities like smuggling and prostitution.

The status of the Kaliningrad *oblast,* which is now completely cut off by Poland and Lithuania from the Russian Federation, as a special military district, with a large military and naval garrison still remains open. Germany has become involved in the old east Prussian region of Koenigsberg in two ways. Firstly, the Russians have attempted to encourage German investment in an effort to turn the, otherwise isolated, region into a special duty-free economic zone, a type of Baltic Hong Kong. They also threatened to resettle Volga and Central Asian ethnic Germans there in the early 1990s but most eventually emigrated to Germany. An agreement on collaboration between Poland's north-eastern provinces and Kaliningrad was signed in Warsaw in October 1992 but not developed in detail. Kaliningrad's future remains open but its fate is entirely dependent on the continent's general development. Russian pressure for an extra-territorial road to it through Poland's north-eastern provinces was strongly resisted in the early and mid 1990s, both for historical and strategic reasons.

Lithuania

Although Poland's eastern border is not questioned by the parties on either side sensitive problems have arisen over their respective national minorities and over attitudes towards Russia. In the case of Lithuania Poland supported her sovereignty and independence very warmly. Their border was confirmed mutually from the outset even before the establishment of diplomatic relations in September 1991. This was followed on the official state level by the signing of a friendly relations and collaboration declaration in January 1992 which turned into a full treaty signed in Vilnius in April 1994. Problems, however, arose on the level of minorities and what one might call national psychologies. Poles harbour sympathetic feelings for the Lithuanians but this is not reciprocated. The latter see Poland as an historically dominant, patronising bully out to assert a superior culture and language. They do not share Polish sentiments about Mickiewicz and the *kresy.* Piłsudski's seizure of Vilnius and the interwar controversy has not been forgotten. Lithuanian nationalism, therefore, still has a strong anti-Polish emotional aspect which, initially, clouded their common political interests relative to Russia and regional security and economic collaboration.[23]

This explains why the Polish minority in Lithuania has proved such a sensitive sore in their relations. Numbering about 260,000 (7% of the population) it is heavily concentrated in the south-east of the country and still makes up 18.8% of Vilnius city. Most of its intellectual elements left in 1945–47 and 1957–99 leaving a community of mainly industrial and agricultural workers only 5% of whom had completed higher education. Despite the historical intermingling of such areas the Vilnius view that they were 'Polonised Lithuanians' is not justified as 85% (1989) consider Polish to be their mother-tongue. A pro-communist faction in the Union of Poles of Lithuania (ZPL) allied, very unwisely, in 1990 with pro-Soviet forces to oppose Lithuanian independence. It even proposed a referendum that their border area should become a national autonomous region with the possibility of either joining Belarus or the Russian Republic. Although Warsaw opposed this, and the ZPL majority moved decisively against such stirrings it is hardly surprising that the new Lithuanian government suspected the Polish community of disloyalty and secessionist inclinations. This bad start made it difficult to respond sensitively to the genuine economic problems and linguistic-cultural, autonomy and self-rule demands of the Polish minority subsequently. Polish run local councils played an ambiguous role during the failed August 1991 Moscow *putsch* leading to the imposition of direct rule from Vilnius and a Polish boycott of the first legislative elections.

Warsaw was careful to distance itself from the pro-communist and pro-Soviet Russian forces in their minority in Lithuania but their bilateral relations were soured by this problem in the early years of Lithuanian independence. Polish minority, schooling and linguistic rights took a long time to assume a normal dimension until the issue of Polish loyalty and Lithuanian citizenhood had been resolved. The demand for a single administrative region for the compactly Polish inhabited areas of Vilnius and Salcinkai was originally countered by Lithuanian attempts to gerrymander electoral districts. After a public dispute between presidents Wałęsa and Landsbergis a useful first step in resolving differences was taken in the form of the friendship and consular convention of January 1992. Landsbergis' replacement by the successor-communist, Brazauskas, in 1993, led to the abandonment of nationalist rhetoric over both territorial and national minority issues. Military collaboration was agreed in June 1993. A second border crossing was opened ahead of the construction of the *Via Baltica* motorway which now links Warsaw with Helsinki through all three Baltic states.

Wałęsa's visit to Vilnius to sign the full state treaty of 26 July 1994 completed the normalisation of their relations. Much delayed elections to the Polish local councils had taken place by then in late 1992; but historical grievances notably the unsuccessful Lithuanian demand that Poland apologise for the 1920 seizure of Vilnius, in the preamble to the 1994 treaty, still remained to bedevil their informal relations. As late as December 1996 though, Lithuanian minister of education, Zigmas Zinkevicius, had to be disavowed by his prime minister for threatening to close all non Lithuanian schools and for declaring that only Lithuanian speakers were state citizens. In practice Poland and Lithuania had sufficient common interests, on both the big and small issues, for subsequent regional and bilateral collaboration to develop satisfactorily. Both presidents were able to describe their relations as 'model' during Brazauskas' Warsaw visit in June 1997.

On the other hand the small 12–15,000 Lithuanian minority, living in the 3 communes of Sejny, Punsk and Szypliszki in Suwałki province has never raised any problems. It has always eschewed political demands for territorial auto-nomy. Warsaw has, therefore, had no difficulty in conceding all their cultural, linguistic and educational demands within the new democratic framework of European standards for national minorities.

Ukraine

As with the Lithuanians, the Poles have mixed attitudes towards the Ukraine which they ruled for much of the Commonwealth period. Chmielnicki's rebellion of 1648, the massacres of Poles in the West Ukraine during the Second World War and a guilty conscience about the deportation of 130,000 Ukrainians from south-eastern to northern and western Poland in 1947 mingle uneasily with perceptions of Ukrainian nationalism's Ger-manophil tendencies and very belated liberation from the Great Russian brother's embrace. Skubiszewski's dual-track policy meant that the Polish government, as against Polish public opinion, was initially slow to back the Ukraine's separation from Moscow. On the other hand Poland has supported an independent and pro-Western Ukraine subsequently to the hilt. Remarkably good, if not very extensive, bilateral relations devel-oped surprisingly quickly given the negative side of their traditional animosities.[24]

The Polish elite on the whole saw the Ukraine as a positive opportunity while public opinion lagged behind with negative attitudes which were easily fed by minority issues fanned by unscrupulous right-wing politicians. Kiev's dispute with Russia over the Crimea and the Black Sea fleet were only symp-toms of Kiev's refusal to support Moscow's pipe-dreams of rebuilding its influence in the post-Soviet space through a Slavic triad or a militarily and economically viable CIS. The mutual renunciation of all territorial claims as early as May 1990 paved the way for Polish support for Ukrainian sovereignty in July. Skubiszewski's visit concluded with a declaration of principles on Polish-Ukrainian relations in October 1990 which took a fuller form in October 1991. Diplomatic relations were established in December 1991 with Poland becoming the first to recognise Ukrainian independence while a full good-neighbourliness and co-operation treaty was signed in Warsaw in May 1992.

Wałęsa and the chief of his presidential National Security Council, Jerzy Milewski, were for a while in 1991–93 influenced by Moczulski's concept of achieving a regional security organisation with Kiev dubbed NATO bis. But this idea was abandoned by the time of Wałęsa's May 1993 visit to Kiev which merely confirmed Poland's westward orientation and the hope that the Ukraine would follow in due course. The visit failed to develop economic collaboration, which was a serious matter as their trade had collapsed and revived much less than in the Russian case. Kiev also showed no inclination to reciprocate the Polish Senate's 1990 condemnation of the Vistula action with a similar statement on the genocide of the Poles in the West Ukraine during the Second World War.

Although there is a 250,000 strong Polish community mainly settled in the West Ukraine it does not have any developed sense of political or linguistic-cultural separateness. A Polish congress was held in May 1990 but only about 14% of the community consider Polish as their mother tongue. Unrealistic figures that the Polish community is really a million strong (2% not 0.46%) merely reflect the extent of ethnic intermingling in the *kresy* borderlands. Demands for autonomy for Lwów (Lviv in the Ukrainian) have, therefore, been far weaker than in the equivalent Lithuanian case although they complicated relations initially with the dominant Rukh Ukrainian reform-nationalist movement in the western region. In practice the Ukraine has fulfilled president Leonid Kravchuk's December 1991 promise that every national minority would have its own schools and the freedom to develop its language and culture.[25] Warsaw also takes a relaxed view of revisionist demands by the right wing extreme nationalist Ukrainian fringe.

The Ukrainian minority in south-east Poland was partially deported to the northern and western provinces by the Vistula action of 1947. They were subsequently kept under tight control by the communist authorities and were only able to organise and to express their grievances after 1989. It is difficult to estimate their numbers because assimilation has taken place and a dual identity has emerged based on the factor of Orthodox religion even in the most resistant rural settlements. The figure of about 300,000 is usually cited but the Union of Ukrainians in Poland are correct in claiming that some hundreds of thousands more are Poles of Ukrainian origins. They are divided into followers of Orthodox and Greek Catholic or Uniate religions. Normal demands for linguistic, cultural and educational rights have raised no difficulties in democratic Poland as Polish governments have been genuinely concerned to use the minority as a bridge to good Ukrainian–Polish bilateral relations on the state level. But the issue of a return to the Bieszczady hills is linked to sensitive problems of property restitution and compensation for the deported Ukrainians or their heirs. The Uniate demand for the return of Przemyśl Cathedral provoked a local conflict over jurisdiction between the Roman Catholic and Greek Catholic rites in 1991. The matter is further complicated by the existence of distinct Ruthenian or Lemko and Bojko strands, whose hard-core is estimated officially at 30,000 (journalists claim 60,000), within the Ukrainian minority. Their spokesman wanted moral satisfaction by having the Sejm condemn the Vistula action;[26] their restitution demands, centred on the return of forest areas, involved the Union of Lemkos in conflicts with the State Forests Enterprise over demands for ecological protection and curbs on felling.[27] As in the Belarusan case an important role in smoothing out relations, on both the bilateral state and the national minority level, has been played by joint historical conferences. Such a conference held in Podkowa Leśna in July 1994 dealt with the historical grievances of the 1918–1948 period; it called for national hatreds to be defused by objective treatment of the facts and mutual understanding. The real watershed was passed by the signing of an agreement during Kwaśniewski's May 1997 visit to Kiev which normalised the Volhynian and Vistula deportation issues by bringing them out into the open officially.[28]

Belarus

Belarus has historically been a quintessential mixed border area, fought over and controlled by Poland, Lithuania and Russia. Although its composition is 79% Belarusan, 13% Russian and 4.2% Polish (418,000 according to the 1989 census) it succumbed to strong and successful Russification during the Soviet period. This explains why the Belarusan language lost out completely to Russian in the towns although a mixed dual language majority patois still exists. The linguistic-cultural and ethnic bases for a distinct form of Belarusan nationalism have, therefore, been exceptionally weak so independent Belarusan statehood has found it difficult to find a rationale for its existence. The Poles, motivated by their memories of the Commonwealth, welcomed Belarusan independence as a consequence of the break-up of the USSR. The Belarusans on the other hand were animated by historical grievances such as Polish gentry rule under the Commonwealth and the partition of Belarus by the 1921 Treaty of Riga. They raised imprecise demands concerning the Belarusan population of between 250–300,000 mainly resident in Białystok province and muttered about the return of the Białowieża Wilderness divided at Yalta. This delayed, but did not prevent, the signing of a good-neighbourliness declaration in Warsaw in October 1991, followed by the establishment of diplomatic relations in March 1992 and a full Good-Neighbourliness treaty signed in Warsaw in June 1992.

Although quite promising, Polish–Belarusan relations developed during the Shuskevic-Kebic period of 1991–93 when the Belarusan state cautiously attempted to strengthen its native roots the situation worsened with the election of Alaksandar Lukashenko to the presidency in 1994.[29] His authoritarian tendencies reversed the slow and tentative moves towards democratisation. He repressed Zianon Pazniak's Belarusan National Front which had much sympathy in Poland and even deported Solidarity leader Krzaklewski from Minsk in May 1996. Lukashenko mobilised anti-Polish prejudices demagogically, both against the minority and the country, in his anti-democratic and Russophil drive and accused Poland of fomenting anti-Belarusan plots in Spring 1977. His pro-Russian policies eventuated in apparently ever closer union agreements and an unclear form of reincorporation but he was left isolated by the 1997 Russia–NATO agreement.

The bulk of the Poles in Belarus inhabit the border provinces of Brest and Grodno. It is claimed that 300,000 Poles make up about a quarter of the population in the latter.[30] They set up the Polish Cultural-Educational Association named after Mickiewicz which turned into the Union of Poles in Belarus in 1990. This body, led by Tadeusz Gawin pressed for linguistic and cultural concessions rather than territorial autonomy. The Belarusans number about 300,000 in Poland, are mainly Orthodox in religion and are heavily concentrated in Białystok province. Younger activists animated a rebirth of their cultural and linguistic activity after 1989; but they only succeeded in electing Eugeniusz Czwykwin to the Sejm in 1991 on an Orthodox label and in winning 105 of the local seats in Białystok province in 1990. They lost out after that to Cimoszewicz's appeal in the SdRP interest who succeeded in turning Białystok into his political fiefdom.

SOUTHERN AND VIŠEGRAD REGIONAL POLICY

The Carpathian mountains have separated Poland historically from her southern neighbours causing the permanent political division of the West Slavs. The Poles made occasional forays into Transylvania and Moldavia but one has to go back to the fourteenth century to find dynastic links with Bohemia and Moravia. In modern times Poland developed more national sympathy for Hungary, with whom she had a greater similarity in temperament and social structure, than for the Czechs who were regarded as germanised Slavs. The latter also had an interwar dispute with Poland over the Cieszyn border region. Poland, Czechoslovakia and Hungary had differing perceptions of who among Germany, the USSR and Italy were their primary enemies in the interwar period. This made significant Central European co-operation impossible in the 1930s although there were proposals on paper for Polish–Czech union during, and at the end of, the Second World War. During the communist period they all became Soviet satellites although the extent of their domestic transformation and economic reform varied as did the form of their exit from communism in 1989. Czechoslovakia progressed least politically and actually suffered invasion from the other two through the Warsaw Pact in August 1968.

In general, though, Hungary and Czechoslovakia were somewhat stronger economically than Poland. They were better placed strategically, as medium-sized nations to re-enter Europe and build democratic capitalism and benefitted from easier access to European structures; above all, they did not have to face anything like Poland's Russian and eastern problems and had more nuanced historical experiences with Germany. The USSR had discouraged warm relations between the individual East European states within its empire. The establishment of cordial bilateral relations after 1989 posed little difficulty. There was an enormous backlog of specific problems, which could easily and rapidly be rectified, such as border-crossings and travel, educational and cultural contacts and economic and transport links. Poland signed a good neighbourliness agreement with Czecho–Slovakia in Kraków in October 1991. Relations with the Czechs have always been correct, although lukewarm, and the Poles had no view on Czecho–Slovakia's break-up. They signed a protocol confirming the binding nature for Poland and Slovakia of all Polish–Czechoslovak agreements signed between 1918 and 1992. Traditional emotional preferences for the Slovaks, as a peasant-Catholic people, had little practical effect once independence was gained in 1993, because of Mečiar's authoritarian and pro-Ukrainian inclinations; historical leanings towards Hungary in the region were also, an insufficient basis, for real partnership.

What was important was that the three Central European states, for once, found it mutually advantageous to establish strong regional links after 1991 for two reasons [Staar 1993, chs.11–12]; firstly, to fill the great power vacuum in the area after 1991. Secondly, to present a common front to the West Europeans in forcing through the principle of EU and NATO extension. Regional collaboration was an important secondary string to their foreign policies during the transitional period in the first half of the 1990s between the fall of communism and the extension of Euro-Atlantic structures into the region. Poland joined the so-called Pentagonale (Austria, Czechoslovakia, Hungary, Italy and Yugoslavia) converting it into the Hexagonale in 1991; the grouping, despite turning into the Central European Initiative (CEI) in 1992, which eventually brought in Slovenia, Croatia and Bosnia, proved a damp-squib, and not solely because of the break-up of Yugoslavia.

Most importantly Poland established a triangular relationship with Czechoslovakia and Hungary through the Višegrad agreement of February 1991 which brought Havel, Antall and Wałęsa together in a much publicised summit. This helped the partners to disentangle themselves from the Soviet embrace more smoothly. A subsequent summit in Kraków in October 1991 produced a common response to the weak form of NACC collaboration offered to them by NATO and America.[31] Trilateral, and with Slovakia's emergence, quadrilateral, collaboration in the fields of intelligence and police collaboration, tourism, educational and youth exchanges and commerce, ecological protection and science and culture proved easy enough to implement. This culminated in the Central European Free-Trade Association (CEFTA), agreed in December 1992, which was envisaged originally as being phased in by 2000. Although Slovakia and Slovenia had joined and most tarffs on industrial goods had been lifted by 1997 Poland's trade with CEFTA only made up 5% of its total. Regional initiatives, however, never became viable alternatives to Europe-wide institutions and solutions.The original benefits of a common front on the really big issues of EU and NATO entry proved shortlived. The partners soon found themselves jockeying for preferential positions on this level.

Although the East-West dimension has dominated Poland's modern history, the fall of communism saw the reassertion of northern and sea links including the revitalisation of Czechoslovakia's and Hungary's *entrepôt* links with Gdańsk, Gdynia and Szczecin and the improvement of road and rail links in this direction. Poland was last attacked from the Baltic by Sweden in the seventeenth century but has had friendly links with the states in this area ever since. Poland joined the Baltic States Council in 1992 thus associating herself with the Scandinavian and Baltic states along with Russia. She also participated in resurrected forms of the Hanseatic League.

DOMESTIC FRAMEWORK FOR POLISH FOREIGN AND SECURITY POLICY

The Round Table contract established a shared framework for foreign and national security policy making between the president and parliament. Jaruzelski and his communist ministers, Siwicki at defence and Kiszczak at the interior were originally accepted as shields behind which Mazowiecki's Solidarity led government could begin Poland's domestic transformation. By Summer 1990 they were no longer necessary. The new directing personel carried on a certain amount of self-limitation in dismantling the ersthwhile Soviet control organisations in Eastern Europe and over the withdrawal of Soviet troops from Poland. It took the failed Moscow *coup* of August 1991, the collapse of communism and the break-up of the USSR to bring about the full assertion of Poland's sovereignty which coincided with the election of a fully free Sejm.

The issue of mixed presidential-parliamentary control, however, remained and was written into the 'Little Constitution'. The result was the bitter conflict between Wałęsa and Olszewski in 1992 over who was to control the military forces and set guidelines for foreign policy. A *modus vivendi* between the government and the presidential office emerged under Suchocka and a more political form of cohabitation with Pawlak's and Oleksy's left-peasant majority elected in 1993. Kwaśniewski's victory changed the political balance in the president's favour for two years but he then had to cohabit with the Solidarity majority; by then, however, many institutional mechanisms and conventions had been well established.

Democratic Poland has had five foreign ministers who have assured continuity in this field; Krzysztof Skubiszewski, September 1989–October 1993, Andrzej Olechowski, November 1993–March 1995, Władysław Bartoszewski, March 1995–February 1996, Dariusz Rosati, February 1996–October 1997, and the Solidarity stalwart, Bronisław Geremek after that. Skubiszewski established the tradition of bipartisan foreign policy and of the autonomy of the ministry of foreign affairs (MSZ). Although the historian Bartoszewski was waspishly virulent against the successor-communists, Olechowski and Rosati were both forward-looking professionals who brought Skubiszewski's *westpolitik* to fruition by achieving agreement to EU and NATO entry. The widespread party concensus on foreign policy did not, however, exclude the continuation of institutional and personal scraps over influence between the Belweder, the MSZ and the Sejm and Senate.

The principle of parliamentary control was exercised in the Polish tradition, by powerful committees in both the Sejm and Senate. The most influential in the Sejm were those on Foreign Affairs (chaired by Geremek from 1991 onwards), National Defence (chaired by SdRP general-secretary, Jerzy Szmajdziński after 1993), National and Ethnic Minorities (chaired by Jacek Kuroń after 1993), Poles Abroad (chaired by Moczulski after 1993) and European Affairs (chaired by Jan Borkowski PSL, after 1993). The Senate had permanent committees on Foreign Affairs, Emigration and Poles Abroad and National Defence and a special committee on European Integration Affairs. These committees were mini-parliaments who held their own debates, questioned ministers, civil servants and experts and established their own sub-committees of inquiry and to cover specific fields. Many of their members eventually achieved ministerial or deputy-ministerial office.

The Senate also established research institutes such as the International Studies Centre (OSM), which particularly during 1989–91 acted as centres of Solidarity pro-Western and anti-Soviet initiatives. They balanced the Polish Institute of International Affairs (PISM) which took some time to reorganise and close down in the early 1990s. Its previously dominating academic role in this field was challenged by new institutes of the Polish Academy of Sciences (PAN) and newly established university departments of international relations. The Senate was also freer than the Sejm to express symbolic declarations such as the condemnation of the Warsaw Pact invasion of 1968 or the 1947 'Vistula' deportation of the Ukrainians.

The post-Solidarity and associated opposition to the SLD-peasant government established a Council of Foreign Relations in August 1996. Chaired by Skubiszewski its 22 members it included numerous 1993–97 opposition notables. Its aims were to work for the foreign policy objectives established in the early 1990s and to check up on doubtful aspects of MSZ appointments. Geremek criticised Rosati for permitting MSZ leaks, for allowing too much political interference over MSZ appointments and for allowing Kwaś niewski to dominate foreign policy-making.

Ambassadors are appointed by the president on the nomination of the foreign minister and after the Sejm Committee on Foreign Affairs has expressed an opinion. The latter's objections are frequent but it has, in practice, almost never rejected a nomination. The communist tradition of appointing ex-politicians and activists as ambassador, nevertheless, continues. Ex-OPZZ chair Ewa Spychalska and Andrzej Załucki, a former PZPR Central Committee *apparatchik,* were confirmed as ambassadors respectively to Belarus and Russia by the Sejm Foreign Affairs Committee in September 1996 despite their controversial backgrounds. Deputy-ministers running the MSZ are also political appointments so the emergence of a fully professional foreign office and diplomatic corps is proving painfully slow. This sector has responded to the post-1989 changes although a proposed reform was shelved in September 1994. Overall, Poland has a comprehensive global presence; she maintains diplomatic relations with 175 countries, has 89 full embassies 37 consulates and 16 institutes of culture abroad and a diplomatic service which employed 1102 mainline staff in 1997. While the MSZ in Warsaw, employed 674 functionaries.

NATIONAL MINORITIES AND MULTICULTURALISM

As we have seen, Poland became overwhelmingly Polish and Roman Catholic in the postwar period with less than 3% of the current 38.6 million population belonging to minorities. The complex problems of the post-1989 reassertion of the Ukrainain, Belarusan, German and Lithuanian communities have already been examined; one might add that other, even smaller, groups like the Czechs, Slovaks, Armenians and Tatars raise no problems. The homogeneous *Polak-Katolik* majority have, however, been accused of ethno-nationalism. This is unfair and inaccurate today because on the official level, as confirmed by the 1997 EU commission 'Opinion', the post-1989 Polish state has done everything that is required to meet European standards of national minority treatment. The second level of party politics and political life compares well with France in terms of marginalising racists and right wing extremists, if one contrasts Le Pen's peak 15% support with Tejkowski's insignificant electoral backing. Critics of the Roman Catholic church's integral nationalist tendencies may have a point but this should be placed in the wider context of the continuing struggle for the secularisation of society, as against the state, in Poland. Finally, primitive racial attitudes and stereotypes are admittedly widespread on the popular level but not unique to Poland. Closed communal and extremist attitudes are, however, being undermined by general elite disapproval, the democratic process of education, free mass media, open travel and growing interchange with other groups.[32]

The single main exception to the above generalisation is, perhaps, the problem of the 25,000 strong gypsy (Roma) community whose numbers have been swelled by an inflow of more exotic cousins from Romania. Much remains to be done, but even this can be regarded as part of a general problem of modern industrial societies. The Roma now have half a dozen associations to cater for their interests. The problem, as elsewhere, is between public and popular reactions to, what are viewed as, coloured outsiders as well as the clash between sedentary and travelling lifestyles.

On the other hand the Jewish Question remains a vexing and sensitive one, both as a domestic issue and as a complicating factor in Poland's international reputation. One cannot even begin to examine the issue in any detail, here, but what is agreed is that the 3 million strong minority in interwar Poland 1) was, politically differentiated into assimilationist, traditionalist, Zionist and left-socialist strands and that it, 2) met with a degree of persecution from right-wing integral nationalist and authoritarian Polish forces during the 1930s. The genocide of the bulk of this community by the Nazis in the Second World War ghettoes and death camps of Auschwitz, Sobibór, Treblinka, Majdanek and the like, and their primary responsibility for this unparalled crime is unquestioned. But although the Jewish community in Poland has dwindled through emigration and assimilation to about

6,000 today, communist anti-Zionism and a Jewish purge in 1967–68, the still unclarified responsibility for the Kielce *pogrom* of July 1946, (which caused about 40 deaths) and bad to delicate relations with the state of Israel until 1989 have all weighed heavily on Polish-Jewish relations. The American Jewish community, and its strong academic representatives in particular, have been offended by what they view as Poland's tardiness in apologising for previous integral-nationalist behaviour and in offering restitution for property confiscated by the Nazis and communists. The latter issue was regulated for Poland's domestic Jewish communities in 1997; the Polish state did everything in the 1990s that could be expected to commemorate the Holocaust. Wałęsa's May 1991 visit to Israel and his plea for mutual forgiveness and the abandonment of attempts to weigh up the balance of grievances led to an improvement in bilateral Polish–Israel relations. But controversies such as the proposal to site a Carmelite convent, and later a supermarket, in the Auschwitz perimeter recurred regularly and with much intensity. A CBOS poll showed as late as 1997 that 37% of Poles thought that Jews had too much influence in political life while 29% were of the contrary view.

Although national hatreds and prejudices have decreased the Poles still have decided preferences, some of which have shifted since the 1989 moves towards Euro-Atlanticism. According to a March 1997 Pentor poll Poles had the greatest liking for Americans (54% pro to 7% anti), followed by the French (52%–8%), Italians (49%–5%), Hungarians (48%–6%), the English (46%–8%) and Czechs (41%–13%). More disliked nationalities were the Germans (32%–31%), Lithuanians (27%–21%), Russians (25%–33%), Belarusans (23%–20%) and Ukrainians (18%–38%). Poland had been insulated by communism from coloured immigration so popular antipathies based on ignorance remain widespread against blacks and Indians, hence the colour prejudice against gypsies. The hardworking and clean characteristics of yellow Asiatics, as perceived in their restaurants and growing housing enclaves, were reflected in perceptions of Koreans ((21%–11%), Chinese (19%–13%) and Vietnamese (18%–16%). A 1994 CBOS poll revealed high levels of aversion towards three ethnic groups; 55% were unwilling to accept a gypsy into their families through marriage, 45% were against Ukrainians and 43% against Jews.

Given Polish sensitivity about national sovereignty it is hardly surprising that the issue of Euroregions patronised by the Council of Europe raised much discussion after Poland joined that body in 1991. The Carpathian one, covering part of the Przemyśl region at the extreme south-eastern tip of Poland, also included neighbouring areas of Slovakia, Hungary and the Ukraine. It was much smaller than originally envisaged, excluding Lwów and the Transylvanian fringe of Romania. Proposals involving Germany in the Pomeranian region around Szczecin and Germany and the Czech Republic in the Neisse region were condemned as threatening another partition of Poland in the 1993 Sejm debate by Jan Łopuszański (ZChN). An interesting side-consequence of democratisation has also been a debate about the need to regionalise the Polish state and to cater for the so-called 'small fatherlands' which reasserted themselves after 1989. Autonomist inclinations in Silesia went back to its 1920s assembly but areas like Kujawy, Sandomierz and the Dobrzański lands also began to develop a regional consciousness.

CONCLUSION

Poland stood at a crucial moment in its modernisation in Autumn 1997. While democracy had been consolidated, question marks remained over its political parties and party-system as well as over the speed at which a wholly fresh political generation, unburdened by the ideological, historical and emotional baggage of the communist period, would be introduced into its public life. The economy and administrative structures, both central and local, badly needed restructuring in order to meet the pressing challenge of the transition to EU membership. With the country's external security position as favourable as at any time in its modern history, and inclusion in NATO imminent, the key question became the following; would the Poles manage their transition to market democracy successfully and would they be able to reconcile their national identity with growing Europeanisation and, eventually, globalisation.

1 Adam Bromke, *Poland's Politics: Idealism vs Realism* (Cambridge Mass: Harvard UP, 19 67). Also his *The Meaning and Uses of Polish History* (New York: Columbia UP, 1987).
2 Cf. John Mearsheimer, 'Back to the future', *International Security*, vol 15, no 1 (1990), pp. 5–57.
3 George Sanford, 'Polish-Soviet Relations' in Alex Pravda (ed), *The End of the Outer Empire* (London: Sage-RIIA, 1992).
4 Adam Bromke, *Stosunki Wschód-Zachód w latach osiemdziesiątych* (Warsaw: PISM, 1989), p.113.
5 *Życie Warszawy*, 13 September 1989.
6 Mieczysław Tomala, *Zjednoczenie Niemiec. Aspekty międzynarodowe i polskie* (Warsaw: PISM, 1991).
7 BBC Summary of World Broadcasts (SWB), EE1594, B/3 of 23 January 1993.
8 SWB, EE/1677, B/9 of 1 May 1993.
9 Cf. MON director Antoni Z. Kamiński in *Polityka*, 30 October 1993.
10 Edward Halizak & Marek Tabor (eds), *Polska w środowisku międzynarodowym* (Warsaw: UW LISM, 1993). Roman Kuźniar (ed), *Krajobraz po transformacjl. Środowisko międzynarodowe Polski lat dziewięćdziesiątych* (Warsaw: Volumin, 1992). Janusz Stefanowicz, *Rzeczpospolitej pole bezpieczeństwa* (Warsaw: Marszałek, 1993).
11 Hieronym Kubiak, Poland: national security in a changing environment' in Regina Cowen Karp, *Central and Eastern Europe* (Oxford: OUP-SIPRI, 1993).

12 *Polityka*, 26 December 1993.

13 Anna Wolff-Powęska in *Polityka*, 13 February 1993.

14 *Droga krajów postkomunistycznych do EWG*, (Warsaw, Sejm Chancellory), BSE Materials and Documents series no 4, 12 January 1992.

15 G. Pridham. E. Herring & G. Sanford (eds), *Building Democracy? The International Dimension of Democratisation in Eastern Europe* (Leicester: Leicester UP, 2nd rev. edn 1997), pp. 183–7.

16 Paweł Bożyk in *Polityka*, 14 August 1993.

17 George Kolankiewicz, 'Concensus and competition in the eastern enlargement of the European Union', *International Affairs*, vol 70, no 3 (1994), pp. 477–95.

18 *Wprost*, 28 July 1996, pp. 17–18.

19 *Agenda 2000 ? Commission Opinion on Poland's Application for Membership of the European Union.* DOC/97/16.

20 Report by deputy-minister Jan Kołtun to the Sejm Committee of Foreign Affairs, no 69, 27 February 1996.

21 Paweł Wieczorek, 'The Polish arms industry in the new political and economic reality', PISM Occasional Papers no 23 (Warsaw, 1991).

22 Ekkehard Buchofer & Bronisław Kortus (eds), *Polska i Niemcy. Geografia sąsiedztwa w nowej Europie* (Kraków: Uniwersitas, 1995).

23 Stephen Burant, 'International relations in a regional context: Poland and its eastern neighbours', *Europe-Asia Studies*, vol 45, no 3 ((1993), pp. 392–418.

24 Władyslaw & Norbert Gill, *Stosunki Polski z Ukraina w latach 1989–1993*. (Toruń: Marszałek, 1994).

25 *Ukraina in statu nascendi* (Warsaw: BSE-Sejm Chancellory, January 1991).

26 Bulletin of the Sejm Committee on National and Ethnic Minorities, no 42, 27 March 1996.

27 *Polityka*, 3 July 1993.

28 *Gazeta Wyborcza*, 22 May 1997, p.9 for text.

29 George Sanford,'Belarus on the Road to Nationhood', *Survival*, vol 38, no 1 (Spring 1996), pp. 131–53: 'Nation, state and independence in Belarus', *Contemporary Politics*, vol 3, no 3 (1997), pp. 225–45.

30 *Białoruś. Czas odrodzenia* (Warsaw: PAP, 1990), p. 75–81.

31 Rudolf Tokes, 'From Višegrad to Kraków: Co-operation, Competition and Co-existence in Central Europe', *Problems of Communism*, vol 40, no 5–6 (1991), pp. 100–114.

32 I argue this case in 'Democratisation and European standards of national minority protection: Polish issues', *Democratization*, vol 4, no 3 (Autumn 1997), pp. 45–68.

Bibliography

Abramsky, Chimen, Jachimczyk, Maciej & Polonsky, Antony (eds). (1986). *The Jews in Poland* New York: Basil Blackwell.

Ascherson, Neal (1987). *Struggles for Poland*. London; Michael Joseph.

Ash, T. G (1985). *The Polish Revolution: Solidarity*. New York: Vintage.

Benes, Vaclav L. & Pounds, Norman, G (1970). *Poland*. London: Benn.

Bromke, Adam (1967). *Poland's Politics: Idealism vs. Realism*. Cambridge, MA: Harvard UP.

Connor, Walter D. & Płoszajski, Piotr (eds). (1992). *The Polish Road from Socialism*. New York: M. E. Sharpe.

Coutouvidis, John & Reynolds, Jaime (1986). *Poland 1939-1947*. Leicester: Leicester UP.

Davies, Norman (1981). *God's Playground: a History of Poland*. Oxford: Clarendon Press, 2 vols.

Dziewanowski, Marian K (1976). *The Communist Party of Poland*. Cambridge, MA: Harvard UP.

Gieysztor, Aleksander *et.al.*(1979). *History of Poland*. Warsaw: Państwowe Wydawnictwo Naukowe.

Gomulka, Stanislaw & Polonsky, Antony (eds). (1990). *Polish Paradoxes*. London: Routledge.

Hahn, Werner (1987). *Democracy in a Communist Party*. New York: Columbia UP.

Halecki, Oskar (revised by Antony Polonsky). (1978). *A History of Poland*. London: Routledge & Kegan Paul.

Kolankiewicz, George & Lewis, Paul (1988). *Poland. Politics, Economics and Society*. London: F. Pinter.

Leslie, Robert F. *et.al.*(1980). *The History of Poland since 1863*. Cambridge: Cambridge UP.

Millard, Frances (1994). *The Anatomy of the New Poland*. Aldershot: Edward Elgar.

Polonsky, Antony (1972). *Politics in Independent Poland, 1921–1939*. Oxford: Clarendon Press.

Sanford, George (ed). (1992). *Democratization in Poland, 1988–1990*. Basingstoke: Macmillan.

Sanford, George & Gozdecka-Sanford, Adriana (1993). *Poland*. Oxford: Clio Press, World Bibliographical Series no 32.

Sanford, George & Gozdecka-Sanford, Adriana (1994). *Historical Dictionary of Poland*. Metuchen NJ, Scarecrow Press.

Staar, Richard F (ed). (1993). *Transition to Democracy in Poland*. New York: St Martin's Press.

Taras, Ray (1986) *Poland. Socialist State, Rebellious Nation*. Boulder, CO: Westview Press.

Taras, Ray (1995). *Consolidating Democracy in Poland*. Boulder, CO: Westview Press.

Węcławowicz, Grzegorz (1996). *Contemporary Poland: Space and Society*. London: UCL Press.

Zamoyski, Adam (1987). *The Polish Way: a Thousand Year History of the Poles and their Culture*. London: John Murray.

Index